# simply good food

# simply good food

**Clare Ferguson** with photography by **Peter Cassidy** and **Jeremy Hopley**

RYLAND
PETERS
& SMALL

LONDON  NEW YORK

First published in the United States in 2002
by Ryland Peters & Small, Inc.
519 Broadway, 5th Floor
New York, NY 10012
www.rylandpeters.com

Printed in China

10 9 8 7 6 5 4 3 2 1

Library of Congress
Cataloging-in-Publication Data

Ferguson, Clare.
Simply good food / Clare Ferguson ;
with photography by Peter Cassidy
and Jeremy Hopley.
  p.cm.
ISBN 1-84172-251-0
1. Cookery, International. I. Title.

TX725.A1 F4175 2002
641.59—dc21          20001048752

Senior Designer  **Catherine Randy**
Commissioning Editor
      **Elsa Petersen-Schepelern**
Production  **Deborah Wehner**
Art Director  **Gabriella Le Grazie**
Publishing Director  **Alison Starling**

Food Stylist  **Clare Ferguson**
Assistant Food Stylists  **Fiona Smith,
      Bethany Heald, Pippa Cuthbert**
Stylist  **Wei Tang**

Photographers  **Peter Cassidy**

Pages 2, 4, 5, 6, 7, 8 left, 10, 11, 18, 19, 28, 29, 32,
33, 38, 40 –41, 42–43, 45, 46, 48 right, 49, 50, 51,52,
53, 54, 54, 57, 58, 59, 62, 67, 72 right, 73 left, 75, 79,
83, 90, 91, 93, 94, 97, 98, 101, 103, 104, 105, 107,
108, 109, 112–113, 119, 120, 125, 126 left, 127 left,
132, 138, 139, 140, 141, Endpapers.

**Jeremy Hopley**

Pages 1, 3, 8 right, 9, 12–13, 15, 17, 21, 22–23,
24–25, 27, 30, 34, 37, 48 left, 60, 65, 68, 71, 72 left,
73 right, 76, 80–81, 85, 86–87, 89, 110, 114–115, 116,
122–123, 126 right, 127 right, 129, 131, 135, 136.

Recipes from this book have been published
previously in *Chicken: from Maryland to Kiev,
Extra Virgin: Cooking with Olive Oil, Flavors
of China, Flavors of Italy, Flavors of Mexico,
Rice: from Risotto to Sushi,* and *Street Food,*
all by Clare Ferguson.

## DEDICATION

To Ian, my husband, with love and thanks.

## NOTES

All spoon measurements used in this book
are level unless otherwise specified.

Uncooked or partially cooked eggs should
not be served to the very old or frail, the very
young, or to pregnant women.

Ovens should be preheated to the specified
temperature. Recipes in this book were
tested with a regular oven. If using a
convection oven, decrease the oven
temperature by 40°F, or follow the
manufacturer's instructions.

# contents

Are you short of time, but still want to cook good things? Remember, good fresh food, quickly cooked, can take less time than heating up a precooked supermarket frozen meal. These are my favorite easy recipes. Some are perfect for quick family meals, some are more spectacular for when you have friends for dinner, and some make perfect party food.

# Simply good food …

What makes cooking relaxed and fun is having confidence and enjoying the whole process—getting a lively food idea, shopping, preparing, and cooking it effectively, serving the dish with pride, then, finally, eating it with pleasure.

How do we make every snack, every meal, effortless and good? I start with a pantry of basics that lets me add spice, verve, and flavor to other dishes. Staples like rice, noodles, and pasta are important—I keep several kinds of each on hand. I buy my favorite spices in small quantities (they lose their flavor over time). I also keep some special treats, like dried mushrooms, canned anchovies, sun-dried tomatoes, and peppers, all of which allow me to give some verve to my cooking. I also keep virgin olive oil, capers, curry pastes, and hot sauces, plus cans of tuna, coconut milk, chickpeas, and beans such as cannellini, red kidney, and pinto beans to save time soaking the dried ones from scratch.

I don't have a freezer chock-full of frozen entrées, but it does contain wonton wrappers, phyllo pastry, Asian flavorings like kaffir lime leaves, lemongrass, grated ginger, even chiles, so I don't have to visit an Asian market every week. Frozen berries, ice cream, and flatbreads are wonderful too.

Back-up ingredients like these make life easy—but, for food to be good, it must also be fresh. Buying food fresh lets you control the quality of what you buy. I make sure my meat, poultry, and eggs are all free-range and organic. My fish is always fresh from a quality fishmonger. Fruit, vegetables, and herbs are better when bought in small quantities often—their vitamins and other nutrients are more viable and better for you when used fresh or freshly cooked.

Given good basic ingredients, cooking doesn't have to be difficult. For this reason I decided to collect many of my best, easiest recipes and put them into this one, user-friendly cookbook *Simply Good Food*. Have fun cooking—and eat well, too.

# appetizers

# & snacks

Some people think frying in oil is difficult, but it couldn't be easier. I use a good-quality oil because it's healthier—olive oil is great, but others like peanut or safflower oil are also good. Make the batter first, then set aside while you prepare the vegetables.

# vegetable fritto misto

**4 zucchini, sliced into thin ribbons with a vegetable peeler**

**8 baby spinach leaves**

**8 sprigs of flat-leaf parsley**

**8 scallions, halved crosswise**

**8 thin asparagus spears**

**8 okra, stalk ends trimmed slightly**

**olive oil or peanut oil, for frying**

**2 limes or lemons, cut into wedges, to serve (optional)**

BATTER

**2 cups all-purpose flour**

**3 tablespoons olive oil**

**3 egg whites**

**¼ teaspoon salt**

**SERVES 4–6**

Wash and dry all the vegetables with paper towels. If using okra, trim off the brown stalk ends only, so that none of the interior is exposed.

To make the batter, sift the flour into a large bowl. Put the olive oil into a second bowl, add 1½ cups warm water, and beat well. Beat the oil mixture into the sifted flour to give a creamy batter, then set aside for about 20 minutes.

Meanwhile pour about 4 inches depth of oil into a deep-fryer or a saucepan fitted with a frying basket. Heat the oil to 400°F or until a ½-inch cube of bread browns in about 25 seconds.

Put the egg whites and salt into a separate straight-sided bowl, beat well, then fold the mixture gently through the batter.

Using tongs or a skewer, dip each piece of vegetable into the batter, then fry in batches until crisp, golden, and vividly green. Remove and drain on crumpled paper towels and keep hot while you fry the remaining vegetables. Serve hot with lime or lemon wedges, if using.

Put the pepper flakes, salt, and orange zest into a bowl and toss gently. Put the oil into a medium saucepan or electric deep-fryer and heat to 375°F.

To peel the plantains, cut off the ends and run the tip of a sharp knife down the length of the plantain 2–3 times. Push your fingertips between the skin and the flesh and pull off the skin. Slice the plantain into long, thin strips using a mandoline or vegetable peeler.

Working in batches, put the strips into a frying basket and deep-fry until golden and crisp. Remove from the oil and drain on crumpled paper towels. While still hot, toss in the chile, salt, and orange mixture.

To make the salsa, either stir the ingredients together in a bowl, or purée very briefly with a food processor or mortar and pestle—the texture should be very coarse. Spoon over the chips or use as a dipping sauce.

**2 teaspoons hot pepper flakes**

**2 teaspoons salt**

**2 teaspoons finely grated orange zest**

**4 cups peanut or corn oil, for frying**

**2 green plantains or 3 large green bananas**

MANGO SALSA

**1 medium-hot red chile, such as Fresno, jalapeño, or Anaheim, or poblano, roasted, skinned, seeded, and sliced**

**½–1 serrano chile (red or green), sliced**

**1 medium mango, peeled, seed removed, and flesh finely diced**

**½ papaya, peeled, seeded, and diced**

**1 small red onion, finely diced**

**juice of 2 limes**

**juice of 1 orange**

**2 tablespoons light soy sauce**

**2 garlic cloves, chopped**

**2 teaspoons sugar**

**SERVES 4 AS A SNACK**

# spicy plantain chips
## with chile mango salsa

Plantains are cooking bananas—if you can't find them, use green bananas, sweet potatoes, or parsnips. Thinly slice the flesh lengthwise using a mandoline or vegetable peeler so they curl into long loops.

# french fries with mayonnaise

Homemade French fries are easy to make, taste great, and are better for you than most takeout varieties. I prefer to use olive oil, because it really is the healthiest option, but peanut oil is good because it is virtually tasteless. The secret to producing good fries is to cook them twice.

about 2 cups homemade mayonnaise, to serve (page 43)

2 lb. baking potatoes

olive oil and peanut oil, mixed, for frying

salt and freshly ground black pepper

SERVES 4

Make the mayonnaise according to the recipe on page 43.

To make the French fries, cut the potatoes lengthwise into ⅛-inch slices, then cut the slices crosswise to make ⅛-inch matchsticks. Put into ice water. When ready to cook, drain and pat very dry on paper towels or a clean cloth.

Fill a saucepan or electric deep-fryer one-third full of oil, then heat to 375°F or until a cube of bread browns in 30 seconds. Half-fill a frying basket with the matchstick potatoes, lower into the oil, and cook until light-brown, about 4 minutes. Remove and drain on crumpled paper towels. Repeat until all the potatoes have been cooked.

Skim and reheat the oil to the same temperature. Add the potatoes and cook a second time until very crisp, about 2 minutes. Remove, drain, and keep hot. Repeat until all are cooked. Sprinkle with salt and pepper and serve with a large spoonful of mayonnaise.

The Spanish tortilla is a chunky omelet, thick with potatoes, onions, and red bell peppers. Like all omelets, it's simplicity itself. Serve it as a substantial lunch dish—or cut it into cubes and serve as finger food at a party. Everyone loves it—and it's a great way to please your vegetarian guests.

**¼ cup extra virgin olive oil**

**1½ lb. potatoes, halved lengthwise and thickly sliced**

**2–3 Spanish onions, sliced, about 1 lb.**

**1 red bell pepper, cored and diced (optional)**

**6 eggs**

**salt and freshly ground black pepper**

**SERVES 6–8**

# spanish potato tortilla

Heat 2 tablespoons of the oil in a large, heavy-bottom skillet. Add the potatoes, onions, and bell pepper, if using, and sauté over medium heat for 25–30 minutes or until tender, covering the skillet for the last 10 minutes, stirring occasionally.

Put the eggs, salt, and pepper into a bowl and lightly beat with a fork. Using a slotted spoon, transfer the potato mixture into the bowl and stir briefly.

Add 1 tablespoon of the oil to the skillet and heat until very hot. Quickly pour in the egg and potato mixture and reduce the heat to medium. Let the omelet cook, undisturbed, until the base is deep golden and firm, about 5–6 minutes.

Slide out the omelet onto an oiled plate, then put the skillet upside down over the plate and quickly invert the two. Slowly pour the last measure of oil down the sides of the skillet and under the omelet. Cook over high heat until firm and golden—about 5 minutes. Remove from the heat and slide the tortilla onto a serving plate.

Cool a little, then cut into cubes or wedges and eat while still warm.

Antipasti doesn't have to be full-blown Italian. This kind of fresh, easy-to-assemble appetizer is a favorite in my native New Zealand, where the ingredients aren't always Mediterranean, but can incorporate the fresh Asian flavors so popular there. Don't be afraid to create your own combinations.

# modern antipasti platter

Prepare either a large serving platter or 4 plates and arrange a row of goat cheese or mozzarella, caperberries or capers, fennel, and crawfish or shrimp. Add a second row of nuts or olives, cured ham, and figs. (Arrange each one in small piles, twists, or stacks.)

Put the tomatoes onto an oiled baking tray and roast in a preheated oven at 425°F for 8–10 minutes or until blistered, soft, dark, and aromatic. Add to the second row on the platter.

Put the fish sauce or soy sauce into a bowl, add half the oil and half the mint, then mash together. Trickle the mixture over the cheese, caperberries, fennel, and crawfish or shrimp, then sprinkle with the remaining herbs, then the sesame seeds.

Use the remaining olive oil to drizzle over the nuts or olives, cured ham, figs, and roasted tomatoes. Serve cool within 30 minutes.

½ cup mild goat cheese or fresh mozzarella, about 4–5 oz., sliced or torn

¼ cup caperberries or capers, rinsed

1 fennel bulb, finely sliced lengthwise

4 cooked crawfish or jumbo shrimp, in the shell

¼ cup salted macadamias, pistachios, or black olives

4 slices cured ham, such as prosciutto

4 fresh figs, halved lengthwise

4 bunches of cherry tomatoes

leaves from a small bunch of mint

2 teaspoons fish sauce or soy sauce

½ cup extra virgin olive oil

1 tablespoon toasted sesame seeds

**SERVES 4**

Tiny, delicious, bite-size fish cakes make perfect, easy finger food. They are an essential taste of Thailand, yet have now traveled all over Europe and America. Use whatever fish you like—white fish, salmon, or trout are all good.

# spicy thai fish cakes

2 lb. fish, such as salmon or trout, skinned, boned, and cubed

8 shallots or small red onions

2 inches fresh ginger, finely chopped (optional)

1 stalk of lemongrass, finely sliced

¾ cup chopped fresh cilantro leaves

4 garlic cloves, chopped

4 kaffir lime leaves, sliced hair-thin

1 tablespoon sugar

1 tablespoon fish sauce or soy sauce

8 oz. thin asparagus, finely sliced

salt and freshly ground black pepper

peanut oil, for brushing

chile sauce or lime wedges, to serve

**MAKES 42: SERVES 6**

Put the fish, shallots or onions, ginger, lemongrass, cilantro, garlic, lime leaves, sugar, and fish sauce or soy sauce into a non-metal dish and let marinate for 30 minutes for the flavors to develop. Transfer to a food processor and work to a coarse mixture: do not reduce to a paste. Stir in the sliced asparagus, salt, and pepper.

Shape the mixture into walnut-size balls, about 42, then flatten into ½-inch thick cakes and season well. Heat a stove-top grill pan or skillet and brush with oil. Add the fish cakes in batches and cook for 1–1½ minutes on each side, or until golden and cooked right through. Serve the fish cakes with chile sauce or lime wedges.

Grilling, using spicy marinades, is a favorite Vietnamese cooking method. These brochettes are pungent and spicy-hot—not for the faint-hearted. In a pinch, lemons could stand in for limes, but limes epitomize fresh Vietnamese flavors better. Fresh herbs and salad leaves are also typical.

1½ lb. boneless chicken breasts or thighs

2 tablespoons green peppercorns

2 tablespoons black peppercorns

1 tablespoon salt flakes

¼ cup apricot preserves

4 garlic cloves, crushed

2 tablespoons fish sauce

grated zest and freshly squeezed juice of 2 limes

TO SERVE (OPTIONAL)

2 small heads of romaine, leaves separated

2 small bundles of bean thread noodles, soaked in hot water for 3 minutes

2 inches cucumber, sliced and diced

a handful of mint sprigs

*12 bamboo satay sticks, soaked in water for 30 minutes*

**SERVES 4**

Beat the chicken pieces flat using a meat mallet or the flat side of a Chinese cleaver: this will also tenderize them. Cut into 1-inch square pieces.

Put the peppercorns into a dry skillet and toast over medium heat, shaking constantly until aromatic but not scorched. Using an electric spice grinder, clean coffee grinder, or mortar and pestle, grind or pound until coarse and gritty. Transfer to a shallow non-metal dish, add the salt, preserves, garlic, fish sauce, and lime juice. Reserve some of the lime zest for serving and add the remainder to the dish. Mix to a sticky paste. Add the chicken and stir until well coated. Push the chicken, 4 cubes at a time, onto the soaked satay sticks.

Preheat a broiler or outdoor grill. Set the chicken skewers about 3 inches from the heat and cook for 4–5 minutes on each side. Serve with a platter of the serving ingredients.

To eat, remove the chicken from the skewers, fill lettuce leaves with noodles and cucumber, add the chicken, then top with mint and reserved lime zest.

# vietnamese peppery chicken

# miniature spring rolls

Spring rolls should be lean, crisp, and refreshing and make effortless party snacks. Serve them with your favorite dipping sauces—I like grated ginger in a little sweetened rice vinegar. Keep the spring roll wrappers covered with plastic while you work, so they don't dry out.

Blanch the bean sprouts for 1 minute in boiling water, then refresh in ice water. Top and tail them, discarding the ends. Put into a bowl, add the other vegetables and the ginger, and mix gently.

Heat the 3 tablespoons oil, add the vegetables, and stir-fry for 1–1½ minutes. Add the tofu, sugar, soy sauce, and rice wine and cook for 1 minute longer. Cool. Divide into 8 portions (each will be enough for 4–5 spring rolls).

Cut each wrapper in half diagonally. Put 1 piece of filling on the long side, a third of the way from the edge. Fold the long side over the filling, then fold over the side flaps. Roll up. Mix the flour and water and dab a little of the mixture on the pointed end of the roll. Press to seal. Set the spring rolls on a lightly floured surface, not touching, until all are made.

Heat the oil to 375°F or a little hotter, but do not let it smoke. Deep-fry the rolls, 8–10 at a time, for about 3–4 minutes. Remove using a wire strainer, drain on crumpled paper towels, and keep hot in a low oven. Let the oil reheat before cooking the next batch.

When all the spring rolls have been cooked, serve with your choice of dips, such as chile sauce, soy sauce, or minced fresh ginger mixed with equal quantities of rice vinegar, sesame oil, and honey.

**2 cups fresh bean sprouts**

**¾ cup scallions, finely sliced**

**¾ cup carrots, finely sliced**

**¾ cup bamboo shoots, fresh or soaked, finely sliced**

**1 cup fresh shiitake mushrooms, stems discarded, caps finely sliced**

**2 inches fresh ginger, finely sliced**

**3 tablespoons peanut oil, plus extra, for frying**

**2 oz. firm tofu, finely diced**

**2 teaspoons sugar**

**1 tablespoon light soy sauce**

**1 tablespoon Chinese rice wine or dry sherry**

**20 spring roll wrappers or wonton wrappers**

**2 tablespoons flour**

**2 tablespoons water**

**MAKES 36–40, SERVES 6–8**

Put the chicken, pepper, and vodka or gin into a bowl, stir well, cover, and set aside while the other ingredients are prepared.

Put the egg white into a second bowl and beat to a froth. Beat in the bacon or cream, then the sesame oil, ginger, salt, garlic, and parsley.

Slowly beat in the chicken mixture, scallions, and water chestnuts until evenly combined, but do not overmix. Alternatively, gently knead it together using your hands (the authentic method).

Using kitchen shears or a large cookie cutter, cut a round as large as possible from each square wonton skin. Put 1 tablespoon filling onto each wonton skin and, using a small spatula, smooth the mixture almost to the edges.

Put the filled wonton into the palm of one hand and cup your fingers around it, pushing the mixture down with the spatula—you will achieve an open, pleated moneybag shape. Drop it gently onto a floured clean surface to flatten the bottom and settle the filling.

Arrange the dumplings, without letting them touch each other, in a bamboo steamer or steamers. Heat a wok or saucepan of boiling water on top of the stove, set the steamer on top, and steam, covered, for 7–10 minutes, refilling the base with boiling water as necessary. Serve hot, topped with cilantro or chives, and accompanied by your choice of sauces or dips.

1 lb. chicken breast, diced then ground

1 teaspoon freshly ground white pepper

2 tablespoons vodka or gin

1 egg white

3 slices bacon, finely chopped
or ¼ cup heavy cream

2 teaspoons sesame oil

2 teaspoons grated fresh ginger

2 teaspoons salt

2 teaspoons crushed garlic

2 tablespoons finely chopped parsley

4 scallions, green and white, finely chopped

4 water chestnuts, canned or fresh and peeled, finely diced

30–45 square wonton skins

sprigs of cilantro or chives, to serve

**MAKES 30–45: SERVES 4–6**

# steamed moneybags

These little Chinese dumplings are incredibly easy to make. Cook them in layers in a bamboo steamer and serve them straight from the steamer as party food. You can serve one layer while the next one cooks.

# baby pizzas

There's nothing better than homemade pizza (once you've tried it, you'll never bother with ready-made again). They are incredibly easy to make—all you need is a food processor. Make them large—or small like these, so everyone can taste a different topping.

**4 cups all-purpose flour**

**2 packages active dry yeast, 1½ tablespoons**

**1 teaspoon salt**

**¼ cup extra virgin olive oil**

TOPPINGS

**1 cup fresh tomato sauce, tapenade (page 47), or sun-dried tomato pesto**

**1 cup wilted spinach (page 66), arugula, or roasted peppers**

**½ cup black olives and/or capers**

**¼ cup canned anchovies, halved lengthwise, and/or toasted pine nuts**

**8 garlic cloves, chopped**

**1–2 tablespoons chopped fresh rosemary, sage, or thyme**

**1 cup mozzarella cheese, drained and cubed**

**1 cup extra virgin olive oil**

**salt flakes and freshly ground black pepper**

*2 baking trays, lightly oiled*
*a round cookie cutter, 2–3 inches diameter*

**MAKES 32–40: SERVES 8**

To make the dough, put the flour, yeast, and salt into a food processor. Pulse briefly to sift the dry ingredients. Add the olive oil and 1½ cups lukewarm water. Process in short bursts for 15 seconds to form a soft mass, not a ball.

Turn out onto a floured work surface, then knead by hand for 2 minutes, slamming down the dough 2–3 times to help develop the gluten. Put the dough into a clean, oiled bowl. Turn it over once to coat with oil. Put the bowl of dough into a large plastic bag, seal, and let rise until doubled in size, about 1½ hours.

Put the dough onto the work surface and punch it down with oiled hands. Divide into 2. Pat and roll out each piece to a circle about ⅛ inch thick. Push dimples all over it with your fingers.

Using the cookie cutter, cut out about 16 small disks. Set them on a baking tray. Top each one with ½–1 teaspoon of sauce, tapenade, or pesto. Add spinach, arugula, or roasted peppers, then a choice of olives, capers, anchovies, or pine nuts. Add garlic, herbs, or cheese. Season to taste and sprinkle with olive oil. Repeat, using the second half of the dough on a second baking tray.

Set aside for 15–20 minutes, then bake at 475°F for about 12–15 minutes or until the bases are blistered and crisp, the toppings aromatic, and the cheese melted. Serve hot.

6 slices light rye bread

6 slices pumpernickel

6 slices rye bread with caraway seeds

4 tablespoons unsalted butter

TROUT TOPPING

2 rainbow trout fillets, skinned

½ cup white wine vinegar

2 tablespoons sugar

2 tablespoons salt

1 red onion, finely sliced into rings

4 cornichons (baby gherkins), sliced

GRAVAD LAX TOPPING

8 oz. gravad lax or smoked salmon

2 teaspoons crushed black peppercorns

6 fresh sprigs of dill

SHRIMP TOPPING

24 cooked shrimp, peeled

chives or sprigs of flat-leaf parsley

2 tablespoons homemade mayonnaise (page 43)

4 lemon wedges

**MAKES 18: SERVES 6**

Danish open sandwiches are like "retro" bruschetta. All you need is good bread—a light rye is traditional. Spread it with a little butter so the topping doesn't make it soggy, then load it up with your favorite things. I've used some storebought seafood toppings to save time, but try this homemade marinated trout as well—it's easy to do and tastes terrific.

# danish open sandwiches
## with three seafood toppings

To make the trout topping, start the day before serving. Put the fillets into a non-metal dish about 2 inches deep. Put the vinegar, sugar, and salt into a saucepan, heat and stir to dissolve, then let cool slightly. Pour over the fillets, cover, and chill for about 12–24 hours.

Just before serving, butter the bread (this will seal as well as helping the toppings to stick). Set several slices of gravad lax or smoked salmon on each slice of rye bread. Add the pepper and a sprig of dill.

Drain the trout, pat dry with paper towels, and slice into wide diagonal strips. Put 2 onto each slice of pumpernickel. Add the red onion rings and cornichons.

Pile 6 shrimp onto each slice of caraway and rye bread. Add chives or parsley, a spoonful of mayonnaise, and a wedge of lemon.

Serve the prepared sandwiches on a board or large platter.

Two great Mediterranean ways with toasted bread—one from Italy and the other from Catalonia in Spain. The essential requirements are a good, rustic loaf and quality olive oil. The tomato and garlic are classic Catalonian, but bruschetta can be topped with whatever you fancy.

# bruschetta with mushrooms and cheese

**8 slices Italian country-style bread such as puglièse, cut 1 inch thick**

**4–6 garlic cloves, crushed but not peeled**

**½ cup extra virgin olive oil**

**1 cup mushrooms preserved in oil, such as porcini, drained and sliced**

**1 cup Gorgonzola or dolcelatte cheese, about 8 oz.**

**salt and freshly ground black pepper**

**SERVES 4 OR 8**

Broil, toast, or grill the bread on both sides. While the bread is still hot, quickly rub the garlic directly over one surface, discarding the skin as the flesh wears down. Drizzle with enough olive oil to soak into the hot, garlicky toasts. Arrange the mushroom slices over one half of each piece and add a smear of cheese over the other. Add salt (take care: blue cheeses can be very salty) and freshly ground black pepper. Serve immediately.

**Variations**  Instead of the porcini, use smoked artichoke hearts preserved in oil, or top the toasts with 1 cup cooked cannellini beans and 2 crushed garlic cloves, mashed with a fork. Top with sautéed dandelion greens or arugula.

# pan amb tomaquet

Toast, broil, or grill the bread briefly on both sides, so that it is crusty outside, soft inside. Rub one side of each slice with garlic. Pull or cut the tomato into halves and use the cut sides to rub all over the garlic side of each toast.

Top the toasts with loosely gathered folds of jamon serrano or prosciutto. Drizzle oil generously all over each one and serve.

**Note**  You can, of course, finely chop the remaining tomato flesh into tiny bits and scatter them over the top. Or just eat it.

**4 large, thick slices country-style bread**

**2 garlic cloves, halved**

**1 large, very ripe red tomato**

**6–8 slices thinly sliced jamon serrano or prosciutto**

**¼ cup tablespoons extra virgin olive oil**

**salt**

**SERVES 4–6**

# tortilla wraps with fresh green salsa

Wraps are some of the easiest and most casual dishes to prepare. All you need are warmed flour tortillas, then your choice of fillings. This recipe uses refried beans, cheese, and salsa, but you can add grilled meats, roasted chicken, and whatever else you love. Canned refried beans can be made even more thick and spicy if you mash in chopped garlic, then heat in a skillet with extra oil, cumin, chile, salt, and oregano so, they're substantial, hot, and packed with flavor.

**8 flour tortillas, 8 inches diameter**

**2 cups hot refried beans**

**2 teaspoons chopped fresh jalapeño or serrano chile**

**¼ head crisp lettuce, such as iceberg**

**1 cup coarsely grated Monterey jack cheese**

**¾ cup pitted olives, green or black**

**½ cup sour cream**

**8 cherry tomatoes, chopped (optional)**

**sprigs of cilantro (optional)**

**2 fresh red chiles, chopped (optional)**

FRESH GREEN SALSA

**4 scallions, chopped**

**a handful of mint leaves**

**a handful of coriander leaves**

**2 teaspoons salt**

**8 whole allspice or black peppercorns, crushed**

**freshly squeezed juice of 1 lime**

**MAKES 8**

To make the salsa, put the scallions, cilantro, mint, salt, allspice or pepper, and lime juice into a bowl. Mix, chill, and use within 2 days.

To soften the tortillas, spray them with a little water, wrap in foil, and put into a preheated oven at 350°F for about 10–12 minutes until warm and pliable. Alternatively, wrap in parchment paper and microwave on high for 3–4 minutes, or wrap in foil and heat in a bamboo steamer over boiling water for 5–10 minutes.

Spread 2–3 tablespoons of the refried beans on each tortilla. Add the chopped chile, lettuce, cheese, olives, salsa, and cream, fold up the base of the tortilla, then fold over the 2 sides, like an envelope. Serve warm, with cherry tomatoes, cilantro, or chiles, if using.

1 cup quick-cook "instant" polenta or yellow cornmeal

olive oil, for brushing

6 slices prosciutto

a few salad leaves, such as arugula, watercress, or curly endive, to serve

1 cup Parmesan cheese, shaved into long, thin slivers

about 3 tablespoons extra virgin olive oil, or to taste

freshly ground black pepper

*a springform cake pan, 8–10 inches diameter, oiled*

**SERVES 6**

Cook the polenta, following the package instructions, until thick and creamy. Spoon the mixture into the prepared cake pan and spread the top evenly with the back of a tablespoon. Let cool for 15–30 minutes or until dense and firmly set.

Cut into wedges. If the cake of polenta is very thick, cut it horizontally crosswise first to make two disks, then slice into 6–12 segments like a cake.

Preheat a cast-iron, stove-top grill pan until very hot. Brush the surface of the polenta wedges with a little olive oil, then press them onto the pan and cook for 8–15 minutes (you must heat them thoroughly as well as crisping the crust). Using a spatula or tongs, turn over the pieces and cook the other side for 8 –15 minutes.

To serve, set 1 slice on each plate and drape a slice of ham over and beside it. Add a few crisp salad leaves, sprinkle with black pepper and shavings of Parmesan, then drizzle with olive oil and serve immediately.

# char-grilled polenta with proscuitto

Making polenta used to be a rather time-consuming activity. These days, you can find quick-cook polenta, so it's much faster and easier. Cook according to the package instructions, then pour into a springform cake pan, then let cool and set. Remove from the pan, cut into wedges and cook on a stove-top grill pan. Great with traditional Italian prosciutto.

My mother-in-law, Joyce, taught me the recipe for this simple, semi-smooth pâté. The whole thing can be made in less than 10 minutes. It can be eaten warm, but is usually better cooled and chilled (I use the freezer for speed). Wonderful as a first course, or for parties, and a thousand times better than any of the storebought pâtés.

# chicken liver pâté

Put ½ stick of the butter into a nonstick skillet and heat until melted. Add the livers and sauté over high heat for 2 minutes, stirring constantly. Standing well back, carefully add the brandy and light it with a match. Let flame for 1–2 minutes, shaking the skillet, then add the garlic, onion, salt, and nutmeg and cook for a further 2 minutes until the liquid has almost all evaporated and the livers and onion are golden. (Ideally, the livers should still be pink inside.)

Add the thyme and another ½ stick of the butter and heat until the butter has melted.

Transfer the mixture to a food processor. Blend, in 4–5 short bursts, to a semi-smooth paste. Spoon into 1 large or 4 small china pots. Smooth the surface. Melt the remaining butter. Pour it over the surface, adding a decorative topping of thyme and peppercorns, pushing them into the butter.

Let cool, then put into the freezer for at least 1 hour. Transfer to the refrigerator and chill for 1–2 hours until very cold and firm. Serve the same day with Melba toast or crisp, toasted slices of baguette, or store longer: the flavors improve for up to a week.

**1½ sticks salted butter, cubed**

**12 oz. chicken livers, trimmed and halved**

**¼ cup brandy**

**2 garlic cloves, crushed**

**1 onion, chopped**

**½ teaspoon salt**

**¼ teaspoon freshly grated nutmeg**

**2–3 tablespoons fresh thyme leaves**

TO SERVE

**sprigs of thyme**

**about 20 peppercorns**

**SERVES 6–8**

# sauces

# & dips

# vinaigrette

Fresh vinaigrette is so easy to make, I don't know why anyone ever buys it ready-made. Just put into a bottle and shake, or into a salad bowl and beat briefly with a fork.

**¼ cup white or red wine vinegar (1 part)**

**1¼ cups extra virgin olive oil (5 parts)**

**salt and freshly ground white pepper**

**MAKES 1½ CUPS**

Put all the ingredients into a bowl or screwtop bottle. Beat or shake to form a temporary emulsion. Store in a cool, dark place, since rancidity can occur in bright sunlight and heat. Use within a week—and shake again to mix.

To make a smaller amount—enough for one salad— use 1 part vinegar to 5 parts oil, plus seasoning to taste. If preferred, pour the ingredients into the salad bowl and beat them with a fork. Put the salad on top and leave undisturbed (no longer than about 30 minutes), then toss just before serving.

# mayonnaise

Making real mayonnaise with a hand-held electric mixer is blissfully quick and easy—just 5 minutes. It turns any salad into a feast.

Put the yolks into a medium bowl with high, straight sides and a curved base. Stir in the mustard, salt, and half the lemon juice or vinegar, then beat until smooth. Mix the oils into a measuring cup, then, with the cup in one hand and a hand-held electric mixer in the other, gradually pour in the oil, beating continuously, to form a stiff, glossy emulsion. When all the oil has been added, taste, then beat in the remaining juice or vinegar. Taste and adjust the seasoning. Cover the surface with plastic wrap until ready to use. Best used immediately, it may be also refrigerated for up to 3 days.

**2 egg yolks, at room temperature**

**2 teaspoons Dijon mustard**

**¼ teaspoon salt**

**2 teaspoons fresh lemon juice or white wine vinegar**

**¾ cup extra virgin olive oil**

**⅔ cup light oil, such as grapeseed or safflower oil**

**MAKES 1⅔ CUPS**

# pesto

Make your own pesto in the height of summer, when there are big, strong bunches of basil in the market. Homemade, it's a revelation.

Put the pine nuts into a small skillet, add 1 teaspoon of the olive oil, and stir-fry quickly until golden. Remove and let cool.

Put the pine nuts, garlic, salt, and basil into a food processor and work to a paste. Alternatively, use a mortar and pestle.

Still working, add half the cheese, then gradually pour in half the remaining olive oil. Add the remaining cheese and oil all at once and work or blend one last time. The paste should be a vivid green.

**1 cup pine nuts**

**½ cup extra virgin olive oil**

**6 garlic cloves, chopped**

**1 teaspoon salt**

**1 cup fresh basil leaves, torn**

**½ cup freshly grated Parmesan cheese**

**½ cup freshly grated pecorino cheese**

**MAKES ABOUT 3 CUPS**

# tsatziki yogurt sauce

Yogurt in Greece is so rich, sharp, and solid that it's almost like cheese, not yogurt. If you can't find the real thing, drain plain yogurt through a cheesecloth-lined strainer or mash it with cream cheese or even feta cheese for stiffness.

Grate the cucumber coarsely, put into a non-metal bowl, sprinkle with the salt, stir, and let stand for 10 minutes. Put into a non-metal strainer and press hard to squeeze out the salt and liquid. Do not rinse. Return to a clean bowl and stir in the garlic and yogurt. Spoon into individual serving dishes and sprinkle with a little olive oil. Serve with chopped herbs, black olives, bread, cucumber, and carrots.

8 oz. cucumber, unpeeled

2 teaspoons salt

3 garlic cloves, crushed

1½ cups strained plain yogurt

¼ cup extra virgin olive oil

TO SERVE (OPTIONAL)

fresh mint or parsley, chopped

black olives

bread

cucumber, cut in strips

carrots, cut in strips

**MAKES ABOUT 3 CUPS: SERVES 4–6**

# harissa paste

Harissa paste is an exciting, incendiary condiment. It is sold in cans, bottles, or tubes, but is easy to make yourself.

An hour before making the sauce, reserve 3 of the dried chiles, then carefully discard all the seeds and membranes from the remainder. Put the reserved and seeded chiles into a bowl and cover with about 2 cups boiling water. Set aside until rehydrated, about 30 minutes.

Drain the plumped-up chiles (reserving 2 tablespoons of the soaking liquid) and snip them directly into a blender (wear rubber gloves if you are sensitive to chiles). Chop the roasted red peppers and add to the blender with the garlic, salt, cumin, coriander, and paprika.

Add the reserved 2 tablespoons of soaking liquid, plus most of the olive oil, 5–6 tablespoons. Blend to a smooth, red, creamy sauce. Refrigerate and use within 2 weeks or freeze for up to 1 month.

Use for enlivening couscous or pasta, in vinaigrette or mayonnaise, or stirred through vegetable and lamb tagines.

2 oz. large, dried, hot chiles such as cascabel or kashmiri

2 large red bell peppers, grilled or roasted, then peeled and seeded

4 garlic cloves, crushed

½–1 teaspoon salt

2 tablespoons cumin seeds, coarsely crushed

2 tablespoons coriander seeds, coarsely crushed

2 tablespoons mild paprika

½ cup extra virgin olive oil

**MAKES 1¼ CUPS**

# hummus

A delicious Middle Eastern snack. For 10-minute hummus, use canned chickpeas, but cook dried chickpeas, if you have time.

1 cup dried chickpeas or 2 cups cooked

freshly squeezed juice of 1 lemon

2 garlic cloves, crushed

¼ teaspoon salt

freshly ground black pepper

2 tablespoons tahini paste (optional)

½ cup extra virgin olive oil

TO SERVE

hot paprika

extra virgin olive oil

**MAKES ABOUT 2 CUPS: SERVES 6–8**

If using dried chickpeas, put them into a bowl and cover with boiling water for 3 hours (or in cold water for 8 hours). Drain. Put into a large saucepan, cover with boiling water, bring to a boil, partially cover, and simmer for 1½–2½ hours or until the chickpeas are easily crushable and tender. Drain.

Put the chickpeas into a food processor with the lemon juice, garlic, salt, pepper, and the tahini paste, if using. Blend briefly to a mousse. With the machine running, slowly pour the oil through the feed tube to form a creamy purée. Season to taste.

Serve cool or chilled. You can also sprinkle a little hot red paprika on top and add the traditional trickle of extra virgin olive oil.

# taramasalata

Real, homemade taramasalata is a revelation—quite different from the lurid, tasteless, manufactured variety. Specialist gourmet stores sell authentic smoked or salted cod's roe.

Put the cod's roe, bread, lemon juice, and garlic, if using, into a food processor. Purée in brief bursts. With the machine running, pour in the oil, very slowly, through the funnel, to form a pale, dense emulsion. With the machine still running, very gradually add 3–4 tablespoons boiling water to lighten the mix. Stir in the onion. Serve with black olives, raw fennel or crisp celery pieces, radishes, or lettuce hearts, and some warmed pita breads, torn.

**Note** If making with a mortar and pestle, omit the bread.

2 tablespoons pressed salted cod's roe, uncolored, or 4 oz. smoked cod's roe

1 cup stale bread, wetted, squeezed dry, then crumbled

freshly squeezed juice of ½ lemon

1 large garlic clove, crushed (optional)

1 cup extra virgin olive oil

¼ cup chopped red onion, blanched

**MAKES 1⅔ CUPS: SERVES 6–8**

# skordalia walnut dip

Skordalia is a favorite Greek sauce—serve it with poultry, pork, smoked fish, or with crisp raw vegetables. It's also good as a dip or spread.

**1 cup stale country bread, cubed**

**1 tablespoon wine vinegar**

**½ cup walnut halves, coarsely chopped**

**½–1 teaspoon salt**

**2–3 garlic cloves, crushed**

**½ cup thick, plain yogurt**

**⅓ cup extra virgin olive oil**

**MAKES 1⅓ CUPS: SERVES 4**

Set a strainer over a bowl, then add the bread to the strainer. Pour over hot water, then drain the bread and press it down to squeeze dry. Crumble it into a food processor. Add the vinegar, walnuts, salt, and garlic, then pulse in brief bursts to form a thick, coarse paste. Slowly pour in ¼ cup of the oil and process until creamy. Fold in the yogurt to give a slightly marbled effect. Pile into a bowl. Sprinkle with the remaining olive oil and serve cool.

# tapenade olive paste

This delicious, intense black olive paste is good as a dip or spread for bread, but can also be used as a sauce for fish, or folded through other sauces, purées, or pasta to give a Mediterranean flavor.

**2½ cups salt-cured black olives, pitted (8 oz. after pitting)**

**¼ cup canned anchovies**

**½ cup canned tuna in olive oil, drained, about 3 oz.**

**3 garlic cloves, crushed**

**½ teaspoon dried oregano or marjoram**

**½ cup pickled or salted capers, drained**

**¼ cup extra virgin olive oil**

**2 tablespoons brandy**

**salt and freshly ground black pepper**

**MAKES 2 CUPS: SERVES 4–6**

Put the pitted olives, anchovies, tuna, garlic, oregano or marjoram, capers, salt, and pepper into a food processor. Work to a messy paste, then slowly pour the oil through the feed tube, in pulsing bursts. Taste and adjust the seasoning. Sprinkle in half the brandy and purée again. Alternatively, use a mortar and pestle.

Spoon into a bowl and sprinkle the remaining brandy over the top. Serve with crusty bread, garlicky bread, crostini, breadsticks, crisp raw vegetables, or baked seafood.

**Note** Don't even consider using the pre-pitted, canned, or bottled kind of black olives. Proper tree-ripened black olives, pitted at home, are essential.

# salads &

# vegetables

2 handfuls of peppery leaves, such as arugula or watercress

2 handfuls of bitter leaves, such as chicory, escarole, or frisée

2 handfuls of crisp lettuce, such baby romaine, torn

1 small head of Belgian endive, separated into leaves

leaves from a small bunch of flat-leaf parsley, dill, or mint (optional)

1 small onion, finely sliced into rings

DRESSING

2 garlic cloves, crushed

½ teaspoon salt

1–1½ tablespoons freshly squeezed lemon juice

½–⅓ cup extra virgin olive oil

**SERVES 4**

To make the dressing, put the garlic, salt, and half the lemon juice into a small bowl and mix with a hand-held stick blender. Slowly pour in the oil and blend until a rich emulsion forms. Taste, then add enough lemon juice to give bite.

Alternatively, use a mortar and pestle to pound the garlic and salt to a sticky paste. Slowly pour in the oil, continuing to pound and stir until a rich emulsion forms. Add lemon juice to taste.

Put the washed leaves, herbs, if using, and onion rings into a large bowl, cover with a plastic bag, seal, and chill until ready to serve, so the leaves stay crisp and fresh.

Just before serving, trickle the dressing over the leaves and toss thoroughly with your hands or 2 wooden spoons.

# fresh green salad

A green salad is the easiest of dishes to assemble, but, to be successful, the ingredients must be very good quality. Choose a selection of leaves (soft and crisp, sweet and bitter), then dress with best extra virgin olive oil, the lightest touch of vinegar or lemon juice, and just the right amount of seasoning.

The secret with oranges is to remove all the bitter white pith. Cut a slice off the top and bottom of the fruit, stand it on the base, then slice off the peel from top to bottom. Keep all the juice to add to the dressing.

# moroccan orange salad
## with olives and onions

**4–6 large oranges, about 1½ lb.**

**1 teaspoon harissa paste (page 44) or a dash of Tabasco**

**¼ cup extra virgin olive oil**

**2 red onions, finely sliced into rings**

**about 20 green olives stuffed with anchovies**

**about 20 dry-cured black olives, such as niçoise**

**sprigs of mint, to serve**

**SERVES 4–6**

Wash and dry the oranges and, using a zester or grater, remove about 1 tablespoon of zest shreds and set aside. Using a sharp knife, remove and discard the skin, pith, and the outer membranes.

Slice the oranges crosswise, reserving all the juices. Put the collected juices, harissa paste, and olive oil into a bowl and beat to form a pinky-red dressing. (If there doesn't seem to be enough juice, squeeze one of the orange slices and add its juices as well.) Put the sliced onions into a bowl, cover with boiling water, leave for 2 minutes, then drain. Refresh in a bowl of ice water, then drain again.

Arrange the sliced oranges on a platter. Add the onion rings and olives, trickle the dressing over the top, then add the orange zest and mint sprigs. Serve cool.

An outrageously easy salad—but, as always, best-quality ingredients are essential. Buy very ripe, red tomatoes, extra virgin olive oil, and good mozzarella.

# mozzarella and tomato salad
## with arugula and olives

1 lb. mozzarella cheese

4 large, juicy, sun-ripened tomatoes

4 large handfuls of arugula, about 3 cups

about ½ cup extra virgin olive oil

salt and freshly ground black pepper

**SERVES 4**

Drain the mozzarella. Slice it thickly or pull it apart into big coarse chunks, showing the grainy strands. Arrange down one side of a large serving platter.

Slice the tomatoes thickly and arrange them in a second line down the middle of the plate. If they are very large, cut them in half first, then into semi-circles. Add the arugula leaves down the other side of the platter.

Sprinkle with salt and pepper, then, just before serving, trickle the olive oil over the top. Make sure you have crusty bread (slightly char-grilled tastes good) to mop up the juices. Superb!

**Variation** Sharp, herby black olives may also be added.

Chorizo—Spanish salami—adds extra pizzazz to many dishes. I like to sauté it first to release all the smoky paprika juices. Nothing could be simpler, or have more impact. It's available from many supermarkets and most good gourmet stores.

# warm chicken and chorizo salad

Heat a nonstick skillet or stove-top grill pan, add the chorizo slices or chunks, and sauté gently on all sides until the juices run and the edges are slightly crisp. Set aside.

Put the vinaigrette ingredients into a small bowl or measuring cup and mix well. Use some of the mixture to brush the zucchini halves, then add them to the still-hot pan and cook for 5 minutes on each side or until hot and golden.

Put the chicken into a large salad bowl, then add the lettuce leaves and olives. Sprinkle with the remaining vinaigrette, then add the zucchini, the chorizo and its juices, and the cilantro or parsley. Toss well, then serve immediately with garlic bread, toasted ciabatta, or warmed focaccia.

3 mild or spicy chorizo sausages, about 4 oz., cut crosswise into coin-shaped slices, or a 6 oz. piece, cut into chunks

12–16 baby zucchini, halved lengthwise, about 10 oz.

1 lb. boneless, skinless, cooked or smoked chicken, cut or pulled into long strips

4 cups loosely packed mixed red and green lettuce leaves

a handful of arugula or watercress

16–20 black olives, about 3 oz.

sprigs of cilantro or flat-leaf parsley

VINAIGRETTE

2 tablespoons balsamic vinegar

⅓ cup extra virgin olive oil

2 garlic cloves, crushed

salt and freshly ground black pepper

SERVES 4

# spanish roasted vegetable salad

Serve this easy dish hot, warm, or cool, and with lots of good, crusty, country bread to mop up the juices.

**2 red bell peppers**

**2 yellow bell peppers**

**½ butternut squash or 1 lb. pumpkin, unpeeled**

**2 red onions, unpeeled**

**2 Spanish onions, unpeeled**

**6–8 medium, vine-ripened tomatoes**

**½ cup extra virgin olive oil**

**salt and freshly ground black pepper**

**SERVES 4–6**

Cut the bell peppers in half lengthwise, slicing through the stems. Leave these intact, but discard the pith and seeds.

Slice the butternut squash or pumpkin into 1-inch disks or chunks.

Cut the onions crosswise into halves, leaving the roots and tops intact. Leave the skins on, too—they give extra color and flavor and protect the shape.

Put all the vegetables, including the tomatoes, cut sides up, into a large, lightly oiled roasting pan. Sprinkle half the olive oil over the vegetables and sprinkle with salt and pepper.

Roast towards the top of a preheated oven at 475°F for about 30 minutes, until the vegetables are frizzled, fragrant, and soft.

Sprinkle the remaining oil over the top and serve hot, warm, or cool. Eat the salad with your fingers, discarding the skins, roots, and stems along the way.

**Note** Use bread to scoop up the sweet, oily, sticky juices from the hot pan—superb!

# vermicelli noodle salad
## with duck breast

Dried noodles are a great standby. Some, such as bean thread noodles (also known as cellophane or glass noodles), don't even have to be cooked—just soaked in hot water until softened. Rice flour noodles like these should be soaked first, then cooked for only about a minute. Wheat or buckwheat noodles, made with or without eggs, have to be cooked the longest, but even then only for about 5–6 minutes at the most.

8 oz. thin ricestick vermicelli noodles

3 tablespoons corn oil

4 shallots, chopped

1 inch fresh ginger, finely sliced lengthwise

8–12 fresh shiitake mushrooms, stems discarded, caps sliced

12 oz. smoked duck breast, sliced

1 small head of napa cabbage, bok choy, or Chinese leaves, finely sliced

4 scallions, sliced lengthwise

1 tablespoon light soy sauce

1 cup chicken stock

1 teaspoon sugar

1 teaspoon salt

1 tablespoon chopped fresh parsley

1 tablespoon chopped fresh chives

1 tablespoon chopped fresh cilantro

**SERVES 4**

Put the noodles into a bowl and cover with hot water for 6–8 minutes (any longer and they will soften too much). Drain just before using and, while they are still warm, cut them into half lengths to make handling easier.

Working quickly, heat the oil in a wok, add the shallots and ginger, stir-fry briskly for 2 minutes, then add the mushrooms and duck. Cook, covered, for 1 minute.

Add the napa cabbage, bok choy, or Chinese leaves, scallions, and warm noodles. Add the soy sauce, chicken stock, sugar, and salt. Cook until the liquid has been absorbed—about 2–3 minutes. Serve hot, warm, or cold, sprinkled with the herbs.

Eggplants cook surprisingly quickly, especially when cut into slices and grilled or sautéed. Cook right through: eggplants don't taste good if undercooked, so make sure they have become translucent, with no trace of white.

# eggplant antipasto
## with pine nuts and herbs

**2–3 medium eggplants, about 1½ lb.**

**2 tablespoons salt flakes**

**about ½ cup extra virgin olive oil**

**½ cup pine nuts**

**a small bunch of mint, half chopped, half in sprigs**

**a small bunch of flat-leaf parsley, half chopped, half in sprigs**

**a few drops of aged balsamic vinegar**

**salt and freshly ground black pepper**

**SERVES 4–6**

Cut the eggplants lengthwise into ½-inch slices. Score both sides of each slice with a fork. Sprinkle with salt. Let drain on a rack for about 20 minutes, then pat dry with paper towels.

Meanwhile heat a ridged stove-top grill pan until very hot. Wipe with olive oil using a wad of crumpled paper towel or a heatproof brush. Paint each slice of eggplant with olive oil. Arrange on the hot pan, pressing down firmly. Cook for 3–5 minutes on each side until grill-marked, tender, and aromatic. Heat 1 tablespoon olive oil in a skillet, add the pine nuts, and toast gently until golden. Set aside.

Sprinkle the cooked eggplant with chopped mint, chopped parsley, black pepper, and a few drops of balsamic vinegar. Loop the slices on serving plates, add the pine nuts and sprigs of mint and parsley, and serve as an antipasto.

**Note** If you grow your own eggplants and/or know they are the modern, hot-house-raised, non-bitter type, omit the salting process and continue with the recipe.

Stir-fried vegetables must be one of the easiest dishes of all. The only secret is to have all the ingredients prepared and assembled before you start cooking. The whole process is so fast that you won't have time to prepare anything in the middle of cooking the dish.

# stir-fried greens
## with cashews

Drain the shiitakes, reserving some of the soaking liquid. Remove and discard their hard stems, cut the caps in halves or quarters, depending on size, and squeeze them dry.

Heat the oil in a wok or skillet and stir-fry the cashews, tossing and stirring until dark and crisp. Remove with a slotted spoon and set aside.

Add the bok choy and shiitakes and stir-fry, moving them rapidly around the wok, until crisp and tender. Add the salt, sugar, soy sauce, oyster or hoisin sauce, and sesame oil. Add the cashews, stir in about 2 tablespoons mushroom-soaking water, and serve very hot while the nuts are still crisp.

**4 dried shiitake mushrooms, soaked in hot water for 20 minutes**

**3 tablespoons peanut oil**

**⅓ cup cashews**

**8–12 baby bok choy, halved lengthwise, or 1–2 large, thickly sliced crosswise**

**1 teaspoon salt**

**1 teaspoon sugar**

**1 tablespoon dark soy sauce**

**1 tablespoon oyster sauce**

**1 tablespoon sesame oil**

**SERVES 4**

# wilted spinach

## with garlic, pine nuts, and raisins

2 tablespoons extra virgin olive oil

3 tablespoons pine nuts

2 garlic cloves, crushed

6 canned anchovy fillets, chopped

5 cups well-washed spinach, water still clinging

3 tablespoons seedless raisins

salt and cracked black pepper

**SERVES 3–4**

This easy, delicious dish can be used in lots of ways—piled on top of pizza, as an appetizer, or as a vegetable accompaniment to an entrée.

Heat the oil in a skillet. Carefully add the pine nuts, stir-fry for about 1 minute until golden, then remove quickly with a slotted spoon or drain through a strainer, reserving the oil and returning it to the skillet.

Add the garlic and anchovies to the skillet and mash them together over a medium heat until aromatic, then add the wet spinach and raisins. Toss carefully with tongs or wooden spoons until evenly distributed. Cover the skillet and cook over medium heat for 2–3 minutes, stirring halfway through. Uncover the skillet, sprinkle with the pine nuts, and toss well until gleaming. Serve hot or warm, with small dishes of salt and cracked black pepper.

It can be served with garlicky toasts, sprinkled with olive oil, or in warmed crusty rolls with slivers of cheese. This is also wonderful as a pizza topping, stirred into pasta, or tossed through rice or couscous.

# tomatoes and bell peppers
## stuffed with rice and spices

Stuffed vegetables, such as peppers, mushrooms, and tomatoes, are an easy classic. Leave out the lamb, change the chicken stock to vegetable stock, and the dish becomes a favorite with vegetarians, too.

Scoop the tomato pulp and seeds into a blender. Halve the bell peppers and remove and discard the seeds and membranes. Put the vegetable halves into a roasting pan and roast a preheated oven at 400°F for 10 minutes.

Meanwhile, heat the ghee or butter in a heavy-bottom skillet and sauté the garlic, onions, ground lamb, cinnamon sticks, turmeric, cumin, pepper, and paprika, for about 5–6 minutes over high heat, stirring regularly.

Purée the tomato pulp and seeds in the blender, then add to the skillet, together with the dried cranberries, rice, bulgur, and 2½ cups of the stock. Season with salt. Add the mint and return to a boil, cover, then simmer for 10 minutes.

Spoon the mixture into the vegetable shells and spoon 1 tablespoon of reserved stock over each. Set the sliced tops back on top of the tomatoes. Cover the dish with a double layer of foil and return to the oven. Reduce the oven heat to 350°F and cook for about 40–45 minutes or until the rice is plumped up, all liquid is absorbed, and the vegetables are sweetly aromatic.

Top with the mint and a spoonful of yoghurt and serve with flatbreads.

4 large beefsteak tomatoes, with the tops sliced off and reserved

4 large red bell peppers with stems

2 tablespoons butter ghee or clarified butter

2 garlic cloves, chopped

2 onions, chopped

8 oz. ground lamb

2 cinnamon sticks, crushed

1 teaspoon ground turmeric

1 teaspoon cumin seeds, crushed

1 teaspoon cracked black pepper

2 oz. dried cranberries

½ cup white short-grain, basmati, or other long-grain rice

½ cup bulgur

3 cups lamb or chicken stock

½ teaspoon salt

2 teaspoons dried mint or 2 tablespoons sliced fresh mint

TO SERVE (OPTIONAL)

8 sprigs of mint

8 oz. yogurt

pita or other Middle Eastern flatbreads

SERVES 4

Simple but superb—grilled corn, bathed in a fiery Mexican sauce. The ears can be cooked on a stove-top grill pan or outdoor grill, under the broiler, or even roasted in the oven.

# grilled corn
## with Mexican red salsa

8 ears of corn, with husks and silks

corn oil, for brushing

4 tablespoons unsalted butter, diced (optional)

RED SALSA

2 slices pineapple, fresh or canned and drained

2 large plum tomatoes, halved lengthwise

2 red bell peppers, halved lengthwise

3 tablespoons olive or corn oil

2 tablespoons dark brown sugar

2 chipotle chiles, with stems and seeds

1 teaspoon hot paprika

a small bunch of fresh mint, arugula, or baby spinach, chopped

6 tablespoons pineapple, orange, or lime juice

½ teaspoon salt

**SERVES 4 OR 8**

Heat a broiler, stove-top grill pan, or outdoor grill until very hot. Pull back the husks and silks of the corn and rub or brush the kernels with oil. Broil, pan-grill, or grill for about 4–5 minutes on all sides or until brown, tender, and fragrant. Alternatively, roast in a preheated oven at 400°F for 20–25 minutes.

To make the Red Salsa, put the pineapple, tomatoes, and peppers onto a baking tray, brush with half the oil, and sprinkle with sugar. Roast for 20–30 minutes at 475°F or broil for about 6–10 minutes until slightly charred. Seed and skin the tomatoes and peppers if preferred. Transfer the flesh to a food processor.

Put the remaining oil into a skillet, heat gently, then add the chiles, and cook for 2–3 seconds on each side. Stem, chop, and add to the food processor. Add the paprika, mint, orange juice, and salt and grind to a coarse salsa. Alternatively, use a mortar and pestle.

**Variation** An even easier method is to roast the corn in a preheated oven at 400°F for 18 minutes, add the pineapple, tomatoes, and bell peppers and roast for another 8 minutes, then add the chiles and roast for 1 minute. Remove from the oven and proceed as in the main recipe.

# rice, pasta,

# & noodles

Fragrant risotto, cooked until creamy, soupy, but with *al dente* bite, is comfort food of huge, timeless appeal. Keep the stock hot over gentle heat: the key to effortless success.

# porcini risotto
## with fresh and wild mushrooms

¼ **cup dried porcini mushrooms**

¼ **cup butter**

2 **cups portobello or cremini mushrooms, sliced, or chanterelles, halved**

⅓ **cup extra virgin olive oil**

½ **cup white wine**

1 **cup arborio rice**

1 **onion, sliced**

2 **garlic cloves, sliced**

4 **cups boiling chicken or veal stock**

½ **cup freshly grated Parmesan cheese, about 2 oz., plus extra curls, to serve**

**salt**

**SERVES 4**

Put the dried porcini into a small bowl, add 1 cup boiling water, and leave for 20 minutes to rehydrate. When plump and aromatic, strain and add the soaking liquid to the hot stock.

Put the butter into a large, heavy-bottom saucepan, heat until melted, then add the fresh mushrooms and sauté for 5 minutes, turning and stirring now and then. Remove with a slotted spoon and set aside.

Add half the olive oil to the saucepan, then the rice, onion, and garlic. Cook, stirring, for 2 minutes. Add the reserved porcini and wine and cook until absorbed, about 3 minutes. Add 1 ladle (about 1 cup) of hot stock, letting it bubble up, and stirring gently now and then. Continue adding ladles of stock at 5–6 minute intervals or until the rice is tender and the stock has all been used, about 25 minutes in all—return the cooked mushrooms and add grated Parmesan to the risotto after the third ladle.

Add salt to taste (cautiously, since the grated cheese is also salty). Sprinkle with the reserved 3 tablespoons oil, turn off the heat, and serve, topped with shavings of Parmesan.

**Note** Italian risotto rice comes in many grades; carnaroli and arborio are 2 readily available examples. Risotto rice can absorb lots of liquid (up to 4 times its volume), yet still stays *al dente* as well as creamy. It is delectable.

To make the stock, put all the ingredients except the salt into a saucepan. Add 6 cups water, bring to a boil, and simmer for 10–15 minutes. Skim several times. Strain back into the rinsed pan. Continue simmering for 15–20 minutes. Season to taste.

To prepare the squid, gently pull the head and tentacles away from the body. Cut off and reserve the tentacles. Remove and discard the plastic-like stiffener and soft interior from the body. Remove the skin if preferred.

Discard any open mussels. Put into a pan with the white wine. Boil fiercely, covered, until they open (about 1–2 minutes). Remove one by one and set aside. Strain the liquid into the fish stock, producing about 6 cups total.

Heat half the oil in a large paella pan or skillet. Add the shrimp, langoustines, and squid and sauté briefly until barely set. Remove and set aside. Add the chicken and chorizo, and brown over moderate heat for 10–12 minutes.

Add the onion, bell peppers, garlic, tomatoes, stock, and half the paprika. Bring to a rapid boil, stir in the rice, reduce the heat to a gentle simmer and cook, uncovered, without stirring, for 16–18 minutes, until the rice is cooked.

Add the fava beans, saffron, the remaining paprika, and oil. Stir, add the seafood, then cook for 8–10 minutes on a very low heat until the rice is fully cooked and dry. Add extra stock or water as necessary. Serve sprinkled with parsley, if using.

# spanish paella
## with chicken and seafood

Paella is a great one-pan dish. Use a round, short-grain Spanish paella rice or an Italian risotto rice. Allow two handfuls, or ⅓ cup per person, and cook for about 18 minutes (or 25–30 for calasparra rice, which may also need more water).

8 small squid

2 lb. live mussels, scrubbed

⅔ cup white wine

6 tablespoons extra virgin olive oil

16 uncooked medium shrimp, shell-on, heads removed and reserved for stock (see below)

8 uncooked langoustines

1 lb. chicken cut into chunks

1½ lb. chorizo, cut into chunks

1 large Spanish onion, sliced

2 red bell peppers, seeded and sliced

1 whole garlic head, trimmed

2 large fleshy tomatoes, chopped

2 teaspoons sweet paprika

2½ cups paella rice or risotto rice

8 oz. peeled fava beans

a pinch of saffron threads

⅓ cup chopped fresh flat-leaf parsley, to serve (optional)

FISH STOCK

shrimp heads (see above), if available

2 lb. white fish bones or heads

1 large bouquet garni (sprigs of thyme, bay, flat-leaf parsley, celery, and orange zest, tied together)

2 teaspoons black peppercorns

1 Spanish onion, quartered

2 carrots quartered

1¼ cups white wine

1–2 teaspoons salt

SERVES 8

Good olive oil and Mediterranean vegetables produce an easy, substantial pasta dish. No long simmering here: the tiny tomato halves are oven-roasted and the cubes of eggplant salted, then sautéed, to intensify the tastes. Handfuls of basil are the final flourish. Use any dry pasta—spaghetti, penne, rigatoni, and maccheroni are all good. The sauce is relatively dry and there's not much of it. It is deliberate—it works!

# sicilian spaghetti

1 eggplant, about 12 oz., cut into
½-inch cubes

1 lb. cherry tomatoes, halved and
seeded

½ cup extra virgin olive oil

14 oz. dried pasta, such as spaghetti
or penne

½ cup tomato purée or tomato juice

2 garlic cloves, chopped

salt and freshly ground black pepper

a large handful of basil leaves, to serve

**SERVES 4**

Bring a large saucepan of salted water to a boil, ready to add the pasta when the vegetables are half cooked.

Put the eggplant into a non-metal bowl, then add 1 teaspoon salt and set aside while you cook the tomatoes.

Pack the tomatoes, cut sides up, on an oven tray. Sprinkle with the remaining salt and 2 tablespoons of the oil, then roast in a preheated oven at 450°F for 10 minutes or until wilted and aromatic.

Cook the pasta according to the package instructions (8–12 minutes, depending on type).

Drain the eggplant and pat dry with paper towels. Put ¼ cup of the olive oil into a nonstick skillet and heat gently. Add the eggplant and cook, stirring, over high heat until frizzled and soft, about 8 minutes.

Add the roasted tomato halves, purée or juice, garlic, and black pepper. Cook, stirring, for 2–3 minutes, then tear up most of the basil leaves and stir through. Test the pasta for doneness and drain through a colander.

Return to the saucepan and toss in the remaining olive oil. Divide between heated bowls, spoon over the sauce, add a few fresh basil leaves, and serve.

# pasta with garlic and pepper flakes

Pasta really is one of the easiest of all dishes. To cook it, bring a large saucepan of water to a boil, add a large pinch of salt, add the pasta, then cook at a rolling boil with the lid off until tender but still firm. Garlic and pepper flakes make a simple sauce, while the carbonara variation is one of my favorites too—and not at all difficult.

**12 oz. spaghetti**

**¼ cup extra virgin olive oil**

**1 teaspoon red pepper flakes (peperoncini)**

**6–8 garlic cloves, finely sliced or chopped**

**2 large handfuls of young arugula (optional)**

**SERVES 4–6**

Bring a large saucepan of water to a boil, add a pinch of salt, then the pasta. Cook, uncovered, until tender but firm (*al dente*). Drain through a colander, then return the pasta, with about ½ cup of the cooking liquid, to the saucepan.

Put the oil, red pepper flakes, garlic, and arugula, if using, into a second pan, heat briefly until aromatic, then toss the cooked spaghetti (and the reserved cooking liquid) thoroughly in this mixture, then serve.

**Variation**  Spaghetti alla Carbonara

My favorite version of the Roman dish of pasta with bacon and eggs is based on Elizabeth David's classic. Cook the spaghetti as in the main recipe, but do not drain. Put 2 tablespoons butter Into a skillet and heat until melted. Add 6 oz. chopped sliced pancetta or bacon, and cook until crisp. Drain the pasta and return it to the saucepan. Add 3 lightly beaten eggs to the bacon, stir it until almost set, then transfer into the pasta. Add ½ cup grated Parmesan cheese and toss well. Serve with extra Parmesan.

Homemade pasta is not as difficult as you might think, and pappardelle is easier to make than most, because you cut it into strips with a knife. Elegant ingredients such as lobster, shrimp, or crab will make this pasta an easy, special-occasion dish.

# pappardelle
## with seafood sauce

¾ cup extra virgin olive oil, warmed

1 lb. lobster meat, from 2 lb. whole lobster, or shrimp or crabmeat

a bunch of fresh dill, chopped, about 1 cup

a bunch of fresh chives, chopped, about 1 cup

shredded zest and juice of 1 lemon

salt and freshly crushed black pepper

PAPPARDELLE

4 cups all-purpose flour

5 large eggs

2 teaspoons salt

extra flour or semolina flour, for shaping

**SERVES 4**

To make the pappardelle, put the flour, eggs, and salt into a food processor. Work in bursts for about 1 minute until the mixture comes together in a crumbly mass, then into a rough ball. Knead it firmly together and remove to a floured work surface.

Knead by hand for 2 minutes, then wrap in plastic and chill for 1 hour. Divide the dough into 4 parts, keeping 3 still wrapped. Starting on the thickest setting of the pasta machine, roll 1 piece of dough through, 3–4 times, folding the 2 ends into the middle each time to get a plump envelope of dough, and giving it a half turn each time. Lightly flour the dough on both sides.

Roll it through all the settings on the pasta machine, starting at the thickest, about 6 times in all, until you get a yard-long length of pasta (cut it in half if it's easier). Hang this over a chair or pole to air-dry. Continue the process until all the pasta sheets are lined up. Roll up each length, then slice into 1-inch-wide ribbons (pappardelle). Unroll, dust in semolina flour, then cut each in half, to make strips about 18 inches long. Fill a large saucepan with hot water, add a pinch of salt, and bring to a boil.

Meanwhile, to make the sauce, put the oil into a heavy-bottom skillet and heat gently. Add the lobster, shrimp, or crabmeat, dill, chives, 1 tablespoon of the lemon juice, salt, and pepper. Heat briefly until the flavors blend well. Leave on a very low heat to keep warm.

Add the pasta to the boiling salted water, cook for 1½ minutes, then drain through a colander. Tip the pasta into the sauce, toss gently with 2 wooden spoons, add the lemon zest, and serve in bowls.

Soba noodles are sold in many supermarkets as well as Asian food stores, often next to the ingredients for sushi. Instant dashi is sold in different forms in the same stores, but you can also make your own using kombu seaweed and bonito flakes.

# soba noodles
## chilled japanese buckwheat noodles

**8 oz. dried soba noodles**

DASHI DIPPING SAUCE

**1½ cups hot dashi stock**

**¼ cup soy sauce**

**2 tablespoons mirin (sweet rice wine)**

**2 tablespoons sugar**

TO SERVE

**8 scallions, finely sliced, plus the green tops, whole, to serve (optional)**

**2 teaspoons wasabi paste**

**2 sheets dried nori seaweed**

**1 teaspoon black sesame seeds**

**SERVES 4**

Bring a large saucepan of water to a boil, add the noodles, return to a boil, then add a cup of cold water. Return to a boil again, then add another cup of cold water. Return to a boil for a third time, then drain, refresh, and chill.

Put the dipping sauce ingredients into a bowl, stir well, then divide between 4 soup bowls. Put the scallions into 4 side bowls, with ½ teaspoon wasabi paste beside.

Take the nori sheets, one by one, in a pair of tongs and wave over a low gas flame or hot element until they smell toasty and feel crisp. Crumble or cut into shreds. Divide the noodles between the 4 soup bowls, sprinkle with sesame seeds, add the nori, and serve with scallion tops, if using.

Dried wheat noodles are made from flour and eggs, often sold in tightly packed yellow bundles, usually about 8 per pound pack. They should be soaked in hot (not boiling) water for 10 minutes to soften evenly, then be untangled and added to a saucepan of boiling salted water with 1 tablespoon peanut oil to prevent sticking or boiling over. Cooking time should be about 3–5 minutes.

# combination chow mein

**1 lb. dried wheat noodles**

**¼ cup peanut oil**

**6–8 slices bacon, chopped**

**8 oz. cooked, peeled shrimp**

**¼ cup sweet chile sauce**

**1 tablespoon hoisin sauce**

**4 garlic cloves, sliced**

**1 inch fresh ginger, finely sliced into strips**

**2–3 small heads bok choy, separated into leaves**

**¼ cup light soy sauce**

**SERVES 4**

Soak the noodles, then cook and drain as described above. Heat the oil in a wok, add the bacon and shrimp, and stir-fry until the bacon is crisp and the shrimp are hot.

Add the chile sauce, hoisin sauce, garlic, ginger, and bok choy, then stir and toss for about 2 minutes, until all the ingredients are hot and crisply tender. Add the still-hot, cooked, drained noodles and the soy sauce. Stir-fry and toss until the noodles are well-coated, then serve immediately.

**Note** Some instant dried wheat noodles need only one soak-and-cook stage. Follow the package instructions.

*Mee krob* is the classic Thai dish that ideally requires a large wok, a pair of tongs, and a ventilator fan. But care, optimism and an open window will do—and don't try to cook more than one skein of dried vermicelli noodles at a time. Buy the noodles, rice vinegar, fish sauce, *tom yam* stock cubes, and tiny, fiercely hot, bird's eye chiles from Chinese or Southeast Asian markets.

# crispy thai noodles
## with chicken, shrimp, chiles, and cilantro

Separate the layered skeins of noodles without breaking them. Cook one skein at a time. Pour about 2 inches peanut oil into a large wok and heat to 375°F, or until a single strand of noodle puffs up immediately. Set a large metal strainer over a heatproof bowl. Put crumpled paper towels onto a tray, ready for draining the fried noodles.

Using tongs, add a skein of noodles to the very hot oil. Cook for 10–15 seconds until puffed up and slightly browned, then turn it over carefully with tongs. Cook the second side, then set it on the paper towels. Repeat until all the noodles have been cooked. If there is any dark debris in the oil, pour all the oil through the strainer into the heatproof bowl, discard the debris, and return the oil to the wok. Reheat and continue cooking the remaining noodles. Pour out the hot oil, return the cooked noodles to the empty wok, and keep them warm.

Heat a small skillet, add 1 tablespoon of hot oil, then half the eggs. Cook the omelet briefly on both sides. Remove and repeat with the remaining mixture. Roll up the omelets, slice into strips, and set aside.

Wipe out the skillet and add the sugar, rice vinegar, soy and fish sauces, stock, paprika, and cilantro. Heat, stirring, until syrupy. Add the shrimp and poach until firm. Remove and set aside. Cook the chicken in the same way. Increase the heat, add the bean sprouts, scallions, omelet, and shrimp, and toss gently. Tip the mixture over the hot noodles in the large wok. Turn the noodles to coat, breaking them as little as possible. Add the chiles and cilantro, and serve hot.

**8 oz. fine rice vermicelli noodles**

**peanut oil, for frying**

**3 eggs, beaten**

**about ½ cup sugar**

**⅓ cup rice vinegar**

**¼ cup light soy sauce**

**¼ cup Thai fish sauce**

**½ cup spicy stock, such as stock made from *tom yam* soup stock cubes**

**1 tablespoon mild paprika**

**2 teaspoons coriander seeds, crushed**

**8 oz. uncooked shrimp, shelled and deveined**

**4 skinless, boneless chicken breasts, finely sliced**

**3 cups fresh bean sprouts**

**6 scallions, sliced lengthwise**

**3–4 bird's eye chiles, sliced crosswise**

**a bunch of cilantro, chopped**

**SERVES 4–6**

chicken,

# fish, & meat

# spicy thai chicken soup

One of the world's best-loved soups. Ingredients like lemongrass and kaffir lime leaves are sold in supermarkets as part of the packs of fresh Thai herbs and flavorings. You could use lemon and lime zest instead if you can't find them. Just don't use dried versions from the spice rack—they're just not good enough. Buy extra of the fresh ingredients and freeze them for later.

Put the stock into a large saucepan and bring to a boil. Add the chicken, garlic, lemongrass, fish sauce or light soy sauce, ginger, scallions, and coconut cream.

Return to a boil, partially cover, reduce the heat to a high simmer, and cook for 5 minutes. Add the kaffir lime leaves, if using, the chiles, half the cilantro, and the shrimp.

Simmer gently for 5 minutes or until the chicken is cooked through and the shrimp flesh is densely white—do not overcook or the shrimp will be tough. Add the lime juice and serve in heated soup bowls, topped with the remaining cilantro leaves.

**Note** Remove the chiles before eating the soup: they are fiery, but leaving them whole and merely crushing them releases a gentle, not violent, heat.

5 cups boiling chicken stock, preferably homemade

12 oz. boneless, skinless chicken breasts, finely sliced

2 garlic cloves, chopped

2 stalks of lemongrass, halved lengthwise

3 tablespoons Thai fish sauce or light soy sauce

2 inches fresh ginger, peeled and grated

8 small scallions, quartered

⅓ cup coconut cream

4 fresh kaffir lime leaves, crushed (optional)

2 green bird's eye chiles, crushed

a large handful of fresh cilantro leaves, torn

8 oz. uncooked tiger shrimp, peeled or unpeeled*

freshly squeezed juice of 2 limes

**SERVES 4: MAKES 6 CUPS**

*Do not use cooked shrimp: the texture will be disappointing.*

# chicken kabobs

Small, grilled chicken pieces, sliced and wrapped with herbs, salad, and dressing, must be one of the easiest party ideas known. Flour tortillas, lavash, and pita breads make the best wraps.

Push the chicken onto the skewers and set in a shallow glass or china dish. Mix the oil, oregano, salt, pepper, and lemon juice in a measuring cup, then pour the mixture over the chicken. Let mrinate for 10 minutes. Preheat an outdoor grill or broiler and cook the kabobs for about 5–8 minutes on each side or until the chicken is firm and white right through.

Put the grated cucumber into a strainer and squeeze it dry. Put into a bowl and mix with the yogurt, garlic, mint or parsley, and salt. Gently warm the bread and, if using pita bread, cut in half and open out the pocket.

Pull the cooked chicken off the skewers and divide between the breads, then add the sliced cucumber, tomatoes, lettuce, and onion. Spoon in some yogurt mixture and herb sprigs, wrap or roll up in wax paper, then serve.

**1 lb. boneless chicken breasts and thighs, cut into 1-inch cubes**

**¼ cup extra virgin olive oil**

**1 teaspoon dried oregano**

**½ teaspoon salt**

**1 teaspoon cracked black pepper**

**freshly squeezed juice of 1 lemon**

TO SERVE

**8 inches cucumber, half sliced, half grated coarsely**

**½ cup plain yogurt**

**2 garlic cloves, chopped**

**¼ cup chopped fresh mint or flat-leaf parsley, plus extra sprigs**

**½–1 teaspoon salt, to taste**

**4 flatbreads such as flour tortillas, lavash, or halved pita bread**

**1–2 tomatoes, diced**

**¼ head of crisp lettuce, such as romaine, chopped**

**1 red onion, sliced into rings**

*4 metal kabob skewers, oiled, or 8 bamboo satay sticks, soaked in water for 30 minutes*

**SERVES 4**

Almost all the world appreciates this dish. Stir-fried also means "steam-stirred" in my book, because the vegetables mostly cook in the aromatic steam. Use a sweet chile sauce, not a fiery Southeast Asian version.

# stir-fried chicken with greens

Put the oil into a wok and heat until very hot but not smoking. Alternatively, use a large, preferably nonstick, skillet. Add the chicken and stir-fry over a high heat for 2 minutes, then add the ginger and garlic and stir-fry for a further 2 minutes.

Add the prepared broccoli, scallions, green beans, sliced bell pepper, and chicken stock or water. Cover and cook for a further 2–3 minutes. Stir in the chile sauce and soy sauce. Toss the still-wet snowpeas, sugar snap peas, and bok choy leaves on top. Cover and cook for 1–2 minutes. Toss, then serve while the tastes and colors are still vivid and the textures crisp.

**2 tablespoons peanut oil**

**3 large, skinless, boneless chicken breasts cut into 2-inch strips or cubes, about 1 lb.**

**2 inches fresh ginger, shredded**

**2 garlic cloves, sliced**

**8 oz. broccoli, broken into tiny florets, about 1 cup**

**8 scallions, halved crosswise**

**8 oz. green beans, halved and blanched in boiling salted water**

**1 red or yellow bell pepper, seeded and cut into strips**

**⅓ cup chicken stock or water**

**2 tablespoons sweet chile sauce**

**1 tablespoon light soy sauce**

**2 oz. snowpeas, trimmed and washed**

**2 oz. sugar snap peas, trimmed and washed**

**4 oz. baby bok choy leaves, trimmed and washed**

**noodles or rice, to serve**

**SERVES 4**

# thai green chicken curry

This green Thai curry is now one of the world's favorite dishes. Spice pastes—red, green, orange mussaman, and so on—are an intrinsic part of Thai cooking. This classic green spice paste makes the amount you'll need in this recipe, but you could use it for other Thai dishes as well. If time is short, buy ready-made pastes in larger supermarkets and Southeast Asian or Chinese food markets, but add a handful of cilantro, too. The food processor makes spice mix preparation a work of seconds, but use a mortar and pestle if you prefer.

2 tablespoons peanut oil

4 skinless chicken breasts, about 1½ lb, quartered crosswise

⅔ cup chicken stock

2 cups canned coconut milk

4 oz. Thai "pea" eggplants or diced cucumber

1 teaspoon fish sauce or 1 teaspoon salt

freshly squeezed juice of 1 lime

a large bunch of fresh Thai holy basil or mint

boiled fragrant Thai rice, to serve

GREEN CURRY PASTE

5–6 medium hot green chiles, seeded and finely sliced

a small bunch of fresh cilantro, chopped

2 stalks of lemongrass, finely sliced

1 inch fresh ginger, peeled and finely sliced

4 fresh kaffir lime leaves, shredded hair-thin, or 1 tablespoon shredded lime zest

2 teaspoons coriander seeds, crushed

1 teaspoon cumin seeds, crushed

4 scallions, chopped, or small red onions

4 garlic cloves, crushed

**SERVES 4**

Put all the Green Curry Paste ingredients into a food processor and grind to a smooth paste. Alternatively, use a mortar and pestle. Reserve half the mixture for this recipe and refrigerate or freeze the rest.

Put the oil into a large, preferably nonstick, skillet or wok, heat gently, then add the chicken and sauté for 2–3 minutes or until firm and golden. Turn the pieces over as they cook.

Add the reserved curry paste. Sauté, stirring, for 1 minute. Add the chicken stock and return to a boil.

Add half the coconut milk and the pea eggplants or diced cucumber and cook, covered, at a rapid simmer (not a boil) for 5 minutes. Using tongs, turn the chicken pieces over, then reduce the heat to a gentle simmer. Add the remaining coconut milk and the fish sauce or salt and cook, uncovered, for a further 8–12 minutes.

Add the lime juice and sprinkle with Thai basil or mint. Serve with fragrant Thai rice.

Piri-piri refers to the tiny, searingly hot fresh or dried chiles infused in vinegar, giving a fiery condiment. It is an idea that turns up all over the world and is nice and easy. No chiles? Then add a dash of Tabasco: easiest of all.

# chicken piri-piri

To prepare the game hens or squab chickens, cut them in half down the breast and back using poultry shears. Cut out and discard the backbone. Beat each half out flat with the flat of a cleaver or meat mallet. Pat dry with paper towels. Set on an oven tray with the potato and orange wedges tucked in and around them. Slash the skin twice on the outer curve of each leg (thigh and drumstick). Put the garlic, orange cubes, oil, and salt into a blender and purée for 30 seconds. Pour the mixture over the chicken, orange, and potatoes.

Preheat the oven to 350°F, add the chicken, and bake, uncovered, for 20 minutes. Increase the heat to 400°F and continue cooking for a further 20–30 minutes or until the hens or squab chickens and potatoes are done. (Pierce the meat near the bone—it should be opaque right through, with no pink.)

Meanwhile, to make the Piri-Piri Dressing, put the vinegar, chiles (pierced with a toothpick if fresh), peppercorns, and wine into a screwtop bottle with a plastic nozzle. Shake well to mix.

Remove the hens, potatoes, and orange wedges from the oven, transfer to a serving platter, and sprinkle with the pan juices. Serve the Piri-Piri Dressing separately.

**2 Cornish game hens or squab chickens**

**6 baking potatoes, cut into wedges**

**1 whole orange, unpeeled, half cut into wedges, half into ½-inch cubes**

**4 garlic cloves, crushed**

**⅓ cup extra virgin olive oil**

**1 teaspoon salt**

**green salad, to serve**

PIRI-PIRI DRESSING

**1 cup red wine vinegar**

**1–1½ oz. fresh hot red chiles or ½ oz. dried**

**1 teaspoon black peppercorns**

**½ cup port, Madeira wine, or dry sherry**

**SERVES 4**

# chicken tagine
## with apricots

½ teaspoon ground turmeric

½–1 teaspoon saffron powder

3 lb. chicken, cut into 8–10 pieces

8 oz. dried apricots, about 1 cup

3 tablespoons butter or olive oil

2 onions, chopped

½ teaspoon ground ginger

½ teaspoon paprika

½ teaspoon crushed black peppercorns

1 teaspoon salt

a handful of fresh parsley, tied with kitchen twine

1 crisp apple such as Granny Smith, cored but not peeled, then cut into 8 pieces

mint sprigs, to serve (optional)

**SERVES 4**

This simple chicken dish uses only four spices: two of which are used to rub into the skin of the chicken. If you can't find real saffron powder, double the amount of paprika and use half of that to help color the chicken. The apricots grow plump and juicy with blanching and give the dish a good balance of sweet, salty, and sour flavors.

Mix the turmeric with the saffron, then rub it all over the chicken pieces. Put the apricots into a small saucepan, add 1 cup boiling water, bring very gently to a boil, cover with a lid, then simmer for about 10 minutes.

Heat the butter or oil in a large, flameproof casserole, add the onions, and sauté for 5 minutes, stirring. Add the ginger, paprika, peppercorns, and salt. Put the chicken on top.

Add 1½ cups cold water to the apricots, then pour the apricots and their liquid over and around the chicken.

Add the parsley, bring to a boil, cover with a lid, then reduce to a simmer, and cook, undisturbed, for 20 minutes. Add the apple. Simmer for a further 10–15 minutes, adding a little extra water if it looks too dry (the fruit absorbs much of the water).

Remove and discard the parsley. Serve the tagine with couscous or plain rice, topped with a few mint sprigs, if using.

# provençal roast chicken
## with garlic, lemons, and olives

2½–3 lb. chicken,
preferably free-range

3 tablespoons extra
virgin olive oil

2 lemons

a large bunch of fresh
thyme

1 cup black olives, such
as dry-cured Provençal

4 whole heads of garlic

½ cup full-bodied red
wine (optional)

salt and freshly ground
black pepper

SERVES 4

Roast chicken is everyone's favorite. Add garlic, olives, and thyme and it suddenly acquires all the flavors of the Mediterranean. Easy and delicious, and grand enough for a dinner party.

Pat the chicken dry with paper towels. Rub the skin with a little olive oil and sprinkle with salt inside and out. Put, breast side down, into a roasting pan.

Slice the lemons crosswise in a series of parallel slashes, but leave them attached at the base. Put half the thyme and one of the lemons inside the cavity and push more thyme between the trussed legs and underneath the bird. Push the olives under the bird. Add the remaining lemon to the pan.

Slice a "lid" off the top of each head of garlic. Spread 1 teaspoon olive oil over each one and replace the lids. Brush the remaining oil over the chicken and lemon.

Roast the chicken, breast side down, in a preheated oven at 425°F for 40 minutes. Turn the bird on its back, put the prepared garlic heads underneath, and roast for a further 35–40 minutes until deep golden brown. Prick the thigh at the thickest part—the juices should run a clear yellow (use a metal spoon to check the color). If there is any trace of pink, roast a little longer. Remove the chicken and olives from the pan. Let stand, covered, in a warm place for 8–10 minutes while you make the sauce, if using.

To make the sauce, pour off the juices from the pan. Measure 2 tablespoons of the stickiest, darkest juices and put into a blender or food processor. Add the red wine. Press the soft, creamy centers out of the garlic heads and add to the blender. Tip up the bird and let the juices run into the blender or food processor. Add a quarter of the roasted lemon, pulled into pieces. Blend, in bursts, to a rich sauce. Taste and add water if necessary. Simmer until the raw taste of wine has mellowed, about 3–5 minutes. Serve the sauce with the chicken.

This famous American seafood soup is not at all complicated. Use whatever clams, mussels, and other seafood are available locally. Even canned clams—in or out of their shells—added at the end of the cooking time, will do if you can't find fresh ones.

# spicy clam chowder

Put half the olive oil into a large skillet, heat gently, then add the bacon and sauté until crisp. Remove with a slotted spoon. Add the clams and half the stock. Cover the skillet and bring to a boil. Reduce the heat and simmer for 5 minutes, or until the clams open.

Put wet cheesecloth or wet paper towels into a strainer and pour the clams and their liquid through the strainer to remove the sand. Reserve the cooking liquid and the clams.

Put the remaining oil into the rinsed skillet, heat gently, then add the onion, potatoes, celery, paprika, and chile, and sauté for 5 minutes. Add the tomatoes, remaining stock, and salt. Bring to a boil, reduce the heat, and simmer for 10 minutes or until the vegetables are partially tender. Add the reserved cooking liquid, bacon, and clams, stir gently, then simmer for about 5–10 minutes, until the flavors are well blended. Serve in deep, wide soup bowls, with parsley sprinkled on top.

**Note**  Saltines are traditional accompaniments, but any salted crackers will do. French bread or crusty rolls are also suitable.

¼ cup extra virgin olive oil

4 slices bacon, cut into strips or chopped, about ½ cup

2 lb. live cherrystone or littleneck clams, well scrubbed

3 cups boiling fish stock or chicken stock

1 large onion, chopped

2–4 medium potatoes, cubed, about 2½ cups

3 celery stalks, sliced

2 teaspoons hot paprika

1 medium-hot red chile, seeded and chopped

2 cups canned chopped tomatoes, about 14 oz.

1 teaspoon salt

leaves from a small bunch of flat-leaf parsley, chopped

**SERVES 6–8**

This simple mixture of parsley, garlic, and extra virgin olive oil can create a superb, vividly scented green oil which will make any seafood taste good. Sprinkled over sizzled scallops, shrimp, or fish, it's a sensational recipe altogether.

# grilled scallops
## with parsley oil

Mix the garlic, oil, and lemon juice into a shallow, non-metal dish. Pat the scallops dry with paper towels. Make shallow crisscross cuts in each one, 3 times each way on each side. Add the scallops to the dish of marinade, turning once, and set aside while you prepare the parsley oil.

Put the parsley, oil, and garlic into a blender and blend until smooth. Strain into a bowl or just pour straight from the blender and use this vivid green oil as both garnish and condiment.

Drain the scallops, then thread onto the skewers, 2 per skewer. Pour the marinade into a skillet, bring to a boil, and cook until reduced to a sticky golden glaze. Add the scallops and sizzle them in the glaze for 1 minute each side (or a little longer if preferred). Serve, sprinkled with parsley oil and a separate small dish of oil for dipping. Sprinkle with salt and pepper and decorate with a bundle of chives, if using.

**Variation**  If you prefer to broil or grill the scallops, put the skewers onto an oiled rack about 2–2½ inches from a very hot broiler or grill. Sizzle until firm and golden, 3–5 minutes. Put the marinade into a saucepan, bring to a boil, and cook until reduced to a sticky glaze.

**Note**  Always try to buy unsoaked or "dry" scallops. Don't buy any that are sitting in water. The water soaks into the flesh and the minute they hit the pan the water exudes and the result is a stew, rather than a grill.

**2 garlic cloves, crushed**

**¼ cup extra virgin olive oil**

**juice of 1 lemon**

**1½ cups plump fresh sea scallops, about 16**

**a small handful of fresh chives, to serve (optional)**

PARSLEY OIL

**a small bunch of parsley, finely chopped, ¼ cup**

**½ cup extra virgin olive oil**

**1 garlic clove, crushed**

**salt and freshly ground black pepper**

*8 short wooden skewers or satay sticks, soaked in water for 30 minutes*

**SERVES 4**

# spicy grilled shrimp

This homemade spice mix has lots of flavor, without too much heat. Spices are always better freshly ground—I give a suggested combination below. Alternatively, go to an Asian store where spice mixes are freshly made.

2¼ lb. large, uncooked tiger shrimp, shell-on (about 16)

SPICE MIX

2 tablespoons mild or hot paprika

1 teaspoon kashmiri dried chiles, crushed

¼ cup garam masala*

2 teaspoons ground turmeric

1 teaspoons coriander seeds, crushed

1 tablespoon salt flakes

2 inches fresh ginger, grated

4 garlic cloves, crushed

½ cup ghee or clarified butter, melted

2 limes

MAKES 8: SERVES 4

Soak 8 wooden or bamboo skewers in water for about 30 minutes.

Slash the curved backs of the shrimp, then remove and discard any black threads. Pat the shrimp dry with paper towels. Grind the paprika, dried chiles, garam masala, turmeric, coriander seeds, and salt with a mortar and pestle or spice grinder. Add the ginger and garlic, then grind to a coarse powdery paste. Add the ghee or butter and the juice of one of the limes. Stir well. Rub the mixture into the shrimp, pushing it under the shells so it penetrates the flesh.

Thread 2 shrimp onto each skewer, then broil or grill over a low heat until aromatic: the flesh should be white and firm and the shells pink. Serve with the remaining lime, cut into wedges.

**Note** Garam masala is an Indian spice mixture, sold in Indian and Pakistani foodstores. If unavailable, you can make it yourself, as Indian cooks do. Put 2 tablespoons each of crushed cinnamon, cumin seeds, and coriander seeds into a small skillet. Add 1 tablespoon each of the seeds from green cardamom pods, peppercorns, cloves, and ground mace. Dry-toast to release the aromas, then cool, grind in a spice grinder, and use immediately or store in a jar with a tight-fitting lid.

The only time-consuming aspect of this relaxed recipe is presoaking and desalting the bacalao (salt cod). Its superb taste is the classic base for these fish cakes. You can also use smoked cod, smoked haddock, or even 6 oz. fresh salmon mixed with 6 oz. smoked salmon instead. Put the salt cod, if used, into a bowl, cover with cold water, and refrigerate for 24 hours, changing the water every eight hours. Easy!

Cook the potatoes in boiling salted water for 20 minutes. Drain well, return to the still-hot empty saucepan, and let dry.

Put the milk into a skillet, bring to a boil, add the fish, and poach gently until flaking and hot, 6–8 minutes. Drain well, reserving the hot milk. Cool the fish, then skin, bone, and flake it.

Add the flaked fish to the saucepan, then the extra virgin olive oil, egg, scallions, cilantro, salt, and pepper. Mix and mash to a dense texture, adding ½–1 tablespoon of the hot milk if necessary. Divide the mixture into 8–12 balls. Pat out into flat cakes, then coat in the seasoned flour.

Put most of the olive oil into a nonstick skillet and heat to 375°F or until a ½-inch cube of bread browns in about 35–45 seconds. Cook 3–4 fish cakes at a time for 4 minutes on each side. Using a spatula and a slotted spoon, turn them carefully to avoid splashes. Drain on crumpled paper towels and keep hot while all the rest are cooked, adding the extra oil to the pan. Serve hot with lime or lemon wedges.

**1 lb. baking potatoes, halved lengthwise**

**1½ cups whole milk**

**12 oz. desalted salt cod, or smoked haddock or cod**

**2 tablespoons extra virgin olive oil**

**1 egg, beaten**

**4 scallions, chopped**

**a small bunch of fresh cilantro, chopped, about ¼ cup**

**½ cup all-purpose flour, to coat**

**⅓–½ cup virgin olive oil, for sautéing**

**salt and freshly ground black pepper**

**lemon or lime wedges, to serve**

**SERVES 4**

spanish fish cakes

Steaming a fish is a wonderfully easy idea. This recipe tastes superb, too, and looks beautiful. When serving the fish, lift off the top fillets first, then remove and discard the backbone before serving the rest of the fillets. This is a traditional cooking technique often used in China, Japan, and Southeast Asia.

# steamed bass with leeks and ginger

Pat the fish dry, inside and out, with paper towels. Make 5–6 diagonal slashes right to the bone on both sides of the fish. Rub salt and sesame oil into the slashes and around the cavity. Set the fish on a heatproof dish which will fit neatly into the steamer basket, but still allow the steam to circulate.

Cut the scallions in half crosswise, then finely slice them lengthwise. Cut the leek into similar-size pieces. Peel the ginger and cut it into fine matchstick julienne strips. Sprinkle the leek, ginger, and half the scallions over the fish, pushing some inside the cavity.

Put the fish into a steamer set over a wok or pan of boiling water, cover, and cook at high heat for about 16–20 minutes. Do not let boil dry—add more boiling water if necessary. Remove the fish. Put the soy sauce, rice wine or sherry, and peanut oil into a bowl, mix well, then pour over the fish. Sprinkle with the reserved scallions and serve.

**2 medium bass or similar fish, well cleaned (about 1½ lb.)**

**1 teaspoon salt**

**2 teaspoons sesame oil**

**4 scallions**

**1 small leek**

**3 inches fresh ginger**

**2 tablespoons light soy sauce**

**2 tablespoons Chinese rice wine or sherry**

**2 tablespoons peanut oil**

**SERVES 4**

This spicy grilled pork is eaten with the fingers or with bread rolls or dumplings. Its distinctive flavor is allspice, also known as Jamaican pepper or pimento. Traditionally, jerk pork is cooked over coals made from the wood of this native Jamaican allspice tree, but if you have to use an ordinary charcoal or gas grill or broiler, it will still taste great.

# jamaican jerk pork with herb dumplings

¼ cup tomato ketchup

¼ cup fresh lime or lemon juice

2 tablespoons dark soy sauce

1 tablespoon brown sugar

1 teaspoon coarsely ground black peppercorns

1 teaspoon allspice berries, crushed

½ teaspoon chili powder

½ teaspoon grated lime zest

3 garlic cloves, finely chopped

1 teaspoon salt, or to taste

1½ lb. boneless pork loin, chops, or steaks, patted dry with paper towels

soft bread rolls, to serve (optional)

JAMAICAN HERB DUMPLINGS

1½ cups all-purpose flour

½ cup nonfat dry milk

1 teaspoon baking powder

½ teaspoon salt

¼ cup chopped parsley

corn oil, for frying

SERVES 4

Put the ketchup, citrus juice, and soy sauce into a shallow, non-metal dish, then stir in the sugar, peppercorns, allspice, chili powder, lime zest, garlic, and salt. Add the pork and chill for 1 hour.

To make the herb dumplings, put all the dry ingredients into a bowl, mix well, stir in ¾ cup water, then shape into balls using 2 dessert spoons. Fill a saucepan one-third full of oil and heat to 360°F or until a cube of bread browns in 40 seconds. Fry until crispy outside and fluffy inside. Drain on crumpled paper towels.

Grill the pork over a hot fire for 2 minutes on each side, or cook under a very hot broiler. Serve plain or with dumplings or rolls.

# spicy pork with mexican recado sauce

Many Mexican recipes for pork use a spicy mix to add flavor, color, and sometimes tenderness. Pork can be sliced and used in whatever way you choose: in salad, on rice, in tortillas, wrapped in leaves, or on a purée of sweet potato or pumpkin or with broiled vine tomatoes.

1½ lb. pork loin, cut into 1-inch slices

1½ tablespoons fruit or cider vinegar

⅓ cup extra virgin olive oil

RECADO

1 red onion, cut crosswise
into ½-inch slices

4 garlic cloves, peeled

1 tablespoon hot red paprika

1 tablespoon annatto powder (optional)

1 teaspoon allspice berries

1 teaspoon black peppercorns

2 teaspoons coarse crystal salt

1 teaspoon dried oregano, pan-toasted
in a dry skillet

SERVES 3–4

Pat the meat dry with paper towels. Put the vinegar and half the olive oil into a cup and stir well. Put the meat into a large plastic bag, add the olive oil mixture, and shake to coat. Let marinate in the refrigerator for at least 30 minutes or up to 2 hours.

To make the Recado, put the onion and garlic into a preheated, nonstick skillet or stove-top grill pan. Cook dry (without oil) until toasty, dark, and soft. Put the onion and garlic into a food processor, then add the paprika, annatto, if using, allspice, peppercorns, salt, and oregano and grind to a thick paste. Alternatively, use a mortar and pestle.

Pour the marinade out of the plastic bag into a bowl. Add the paste to the bag, then knead and rub it into the meat until all surfaces are coated.

Preheat an outdoor grill or broiler until very hot. Remove the meat from the bag and broil or char-grill about 2 inches from the heat for 8–10 minutes on each side, then serve hot or cold.

# rack of lamb
## with roasted baby vegetables

Racks of lamb are chined and French trimmed when you buy them—if not, get the butcher to do it for you. The lamb is roasted with baby vegetables and served simply with fresh herbs. Perfect dinner party fare and easy on the cook, too.

**2 racks of lamb, 10 oz. each, Frenched and chined by the butcher**

**1 tablespoon cracked black pepper**

**1 tablespoon balsamic vinegar**

**1 tablespoon sun-dried tomato paste**

**½ cup extra virgin olive oil**

**12 oz. baby new potatoes, scrubbed well and halved lengthwise**

**12 oz. butternut squash or pumpkin, cut into ½-inch chunks**

**¼–⅓ cup red wine**

**4 sprigs of fresh herbs, such as mint, parsley, or rosemary**

**salt**

**SERVES 4**

Pat the lamb dry with paper towels. Put the pepper into a small bowl, add the vinegar, sun-dried tomato paste, and 1 tablespoon of the oil, and mix to a purée. Brush or rub the mixture all over the lamb. Set aside in a cool place or the refrigerator while you prepare the vegetables.

Put the potatoes, cut side down, and squash or pumpkin into a shallow roasting pan. Leave at least a quarter of the area clear for the lamb, which will be added later. Sprinkle the remaining olive oil over the vegetables and sprinkle with about 1 tablespoon salt.

Roast towards the top of a preheated oven at 400°F for 30 minutes. Add the 2 racks of lamb, side by side, with the bones pointing upwards. Continue roasting for a further 20–25 minutes or until the outside is brown, the inside faintly pink.

Remove the lamb from the oven and let it rest in a warm place for 5–10 minutes to set the juices. Add the red wine to the juices and sediment remaining in the roasting pan. Heat on top of the stove, stirring frequently, until reduced to a sauce.

Arrange piles of vegetables on 4 heated dinner plates. Slice the lamb into cutlets, stack 3–4 on each plate with the bones upwards, sprinkle with herbs, then serve with a little sauce spooned around the meat.

Rub 1 tablespoon of the oil into the steak, then rub in the garlic. Chill for up to 1 hour to develop the flavors. Put the remaining oil into a bowl, then stir in the red wine, the balsamic vinegar, salt, and pepper to make a dressing.

Heat an outdoor grill, broiler, or stove-top grill pan until very hot. Put the steak diagonally onto the surface and let sizzle for 2 minutes, pressing down occasionally (the heat must be intense). Turn the steak over and cook for 2 minutes more or until aromatic and firm, though still rare. Remove the pan from the heat, cover with foil, and set aside in a warm place for 2 minutes.

Toss the arugula, onion, and herbs in half the dressing and divide between 4 plates. Carve the steak into thin slices, and keep all the juices. Pile the meat on top of the greens, stir the steak juices into the remaining dressing, then sprinkle over each serving. Serve with crusty country bread.

**Note** Spinach, chicory, or watercress may be used instead of arugula.

⅓ **cup extra virgin olive oil**

**1 boneless sirloin steak, about 2 lb., 1-inch thick**

**4 garlic cloves, crushed**

**2 tablespoons red wine**

**2 teaspoons balsamic vinegar**

**4 large handfuls of arugula, chilled**

**1 red onion, sliced into fine rings**

**a small handful of fresh chives, parsley, or chervil (or a combination)**

**salt and freshly ground black pepper**

**SERVES 4**

# sliced beef on a bed of arugula

Use the best-quality beef available—aged if possible—to produce this tender, grilled, rare steak teamed with bitter arugula or peppery watercress.

Stews aren't complicated to cook—just put them on to cook and they look after themselves. This one makes a useful two-course meal. Serve some of the juices poured over pasta as an appetizer, then proceed to the meat proper as an entrée. Like most stews, it actually improves if made the day before then reheated. Easy entertaining.

# boeuf en daube

Cut the beef into pieces about the size of "half a postcard," as Elizabeth David advised—in other words 2½-inch squares. Heat the oil in a flameproof casserole and sauté the garlic, bacon, carrots, and onions for 4–5 minutes, or until aromatic. Remove from the casserole. Put a layer of meat into the casserole, then add half the sautéed vegetable mixture and a second layer of meat. Add the remaining vegetable mixture, the tomatoes, orange zest, bundle of herbs, and walnuts.

Put the wine into a small saucepan and bring to a boil. Add the Cognac or brandy and warm for a few seconds, shaking the pan a little, to let the alcohol cook away. Pour the hot liquids over the meat with just enough stock or water so that it's barely covered. Put the salt pork, if using, on top.

Heat the casserole until simmering, then cover with foil and a lid and simmer gently for 2 hours or until the meat is fork tender and the juices rich and sticky.

The dish can also be cooked in the oven. Just bring to a boil over a high heat, reduce to a simmer, cover with foil, replace the lid, and cook in a preheated oven at 300°F for 2½ hours, or until very tender.

Remove and discard the salt pork: it will have given a velvety quality to the sauce. Sprinkle with chopped parsley. Serve hot either absolutely plain or with accompaniments such as pasta, mashed potatoes, or rice.

**Note** If using a ceramic casserole dish, brown the meat and vegetables in a skillet, then transfer to the casserole. Cover with a lid and transfer to a hot oven, about 400°F, until the contents come to a boil, about 20–30 minutes. Reduce the heat immediately and continue as in the main recipe.

**2 lb. beef, such as shoulder, cut into ½-inch thick slices**

**¼ cup extra virgin olive oil**

**4 garlic cloves, sliced**

**1 cup thick unsmoked bacon, cut into small dice**

**3 carrots, halved lengthwise**

**12–16 baby onions, peeled**

**6 plum tomatoes, peeled, then thickly sliced**

**zest of 1 orange, removed in one piece**

**a bunch of fresh herbs, such as parsley, thyme, bay leaf, and rosemary, tied with kitchen twine**

**½ cup walnut halves**

**1 cup robust red wine**

**2 tablespoons Cognac or brandy**

**¾ cup beef stock or water**

**2 oz. salt pork (optional)**

**salt**

**SERVES 4–6**

sweet

# things

# italian gelati

¾ cup sugar

1 cup whole milk

4 egg yolks

1 cup mascarpone or other cream cheese

CITRUS FLAVORING

1 cup orange juice (about 4 oranges)

1 cup lemon juice (about 5 lemons)

1 cup clementine or tangerine juice (about 5 clementines or 4 tangerines)

½ cup sugar

1 tablespoon citrus liqueur (limoncello or Cointreau)

½ teaspoon orange flower water (optional)

STRAWBERRY FLAVORING

3 cups ripe fresh strawberries, hulled and chopped

½ cup sugar

1 tablespoon fruit liqueur or dark rum

½ teaspoon orange flower water (optional)

**MAKES 4 CUPS: SERVES 8**

Glorious homemade ice cream is easy if you have an electric ice cream maker. If you don't, just pour the mixture into a lidded metal or plastic container and freeze for 4–6 hours, stirring the edges into the center every hour. The texture will be less creamy, but it is still good. Flavor the basic custard in any number of ways: I've given two of my favorites here, but you could use fruit or nut liqueurs or Italian Strega liqueur.

To make the citrus flavoring, put the juices, the ½ cup sugar, liqueur, and orange flower water, if using, into a bowl, mix well, then strain.

To make the strawberry flavoring, put the berries into a bowl with the ½ cup sugar and the liqueur or rum and orange flower water, if using. Mash to a pulp. Set the bowl in a saucepan of hot water for 10 minutes. Purée in a blender, then push through a non-metal strainer and discard the seeds.

To make the gelato base, put the milk into a saucepan and bring to a boil. Put the egg yolks and the ¾ cup sugar into a non-metal, heatproof bowl, beat to a pale froth, then beat in the hot milk. Put the bowl over a saucepan of simmering water and stir gently until smoothly creamy and thick enough to coat the back of a spoon.

Fold in the mascarpone or other cream cheese, about 1 tablespoon at a time, then stir until dissolved. Put the bowl into ice water to cool, stirring now and then. When cool, fold in the citrus juices or strawberry purée, as well as the liqueur and orange flower water, if using. Stir until evenly mixed.

Churn and serve immediately, or transfer to a plastic, lidded container and freeze. When ready to serve, soften in the refrigerator for 25–40 minutes before serving.

# coconut ice cream

Subtle coconut ice cream with only four ingredients—
five if you count the lime zest. Heaven—and perfect for
serving after any Asian-style entrée.

**2 cups milk**

**1 cup sugar**

**2 cups unsweetened,
canned coconut milk**

**1 tablespoon dark rum
or fresh lime juice**

**thin strips of lime zest
or lime wedges, to serve**

**SERVES 8**

Put half the milk and all the sugar into a saucepan and bring to
a boil, stirring until dissolved. Remove from the heat. Add the
remaining milk and the coconut milk. Cool the mixture over ice
water and stir in the rum or fresh lime juice.

Transfer to an ice cream maker and churn for 25–40 minutes, or
according to the manufacturer's instructions, until firm and silky.

Alternatively, freeze in plastic trays until the mixture is hard at
the edges, but soft in the center. Remove and stir well, then
refreeze as before. Repeat and refreeze.

Serve in bowls, glasses, or cones, topped with lime zest, or
with lime wedges for squeezing.

This Spanish-style doughnut batter must cook in very hot oil, so that the outside crisps and seals quickly and the batter inside is cooked by steam. Add some hot chocolate for dipping and you have a wonderfully indulgent treat.

# churros with hot chocolate

**5 cups self-rising flour**

**½ teaspoon salt**

**1 egg, beaten**

**about 2 cups milk**

**peanut oil, for frying**

TO COAT

**½ cup sugar**

**¼ cup ground cinnamon (optional)**

HOT CHOCOLATE

**1 cup unsweetened chocolate, chopped or grated**

**2½ cups milk, scalded**

*a pastry bag with a ½–1-inch star tip*

**SERVES 4**

Sift the flour and salt into a bowl. Make a well in the center. Beat the egg in a bowl with 1 cup of the milk. Pour into the well and beat into the flour. Gradually beat in enough of the remaining milk to make a smooth, creamy, thick batter able to be piped easily. Transfer the batter to a pastry bag with a ½–1-inch star tip.

Pour a 4-inch depth of oil into a heavy-bottom saucepan fitted with a frying basket. Heat it to 375°F or until a cube of bread browns in 35 seconds.

Pipe long, spiraled, coiled-up lengths directly into the oil. Let sizzle and cook for 4–6 minutes or until golden and spongy, not raw, in the center (test one to check).

Lift the churros out of the oil using the basket or tongs. Drain on crumpled paper towels. Repeat using the remaining doughnut mixture.

When cool, snip the churros into 6-inch lengths using kitchen shears. Put the sugar into a shallow dish, mix in the cinnamon, if using, then roll the pieces in the mixture.

To make the hot chocolate, put the chocolate and scalded milk into a small saucepan, then cook, whipping constantly, until the chocolate is well blended and the liquid is dusky brown. Serve in 4 cups or bowls with the churros.

Serve these for breakfast, or with coffee in the afternoon, or as an outrageously delicious dessert accompanied by thick, plain yogurt.

# crisp honey fritters
## with honey syrup and cinnamon

Put the yeast, flour, sugar, salt, and 1 cup lukewarm water into a bowl and mix well. Enclose in a plastic bag and leave in a warm place for 30 minutes to 2 hours, or until bubbling.

When ready to cook, take a handful of the stretchy, elastic dough. Squeeze it through the bottom of your fist and, with oiled finger and thumb of your other hand, pinch out small, walnut-size pieces onto a plate. Alternatively, use 2 spoons, pincer-like, to pinch out blobs of the dough.

Fill a saucepan one-third full of oil and heat to 400°F—test with a frying thermometer. Drop the dough pieces into the hot oil and cook until a deep golden color, about 4–6 minutes in total. (Flip them over with tongs as they cook.) Open one to test—the inside must be damply soft, not raw. Remove from the oil with tongs or a slotted spoon, drain on crumpled paper towels, and keep them hot while you cook the remainder.

To make the syrup, put the honey and lemon juice into a saucepan and heat until scented. Spoon over the fritters and sprinkle with ground cinnamon.

**1 package active dry yeast, 2½ tablespoons**

**2 cups all-purpose flour, sifted**

**1 teaspoon sugar**

**½ teaspoon salt**

**4 teaspoons ground cinnamon, to serve**

**corn or peanut oil, for frying**

HONEY SYRUP

**½ cup honey**

**juice of 1 lemon**

**MAKES ABOUT 20**

3 tablespoons butter ghee
or unsalted butter

1½ oz. white basmati rice,
washed, drained, and air-dried

2 fresh bay leaves, crushed

8 cups whole milk

½ cup light brown sugar

½ cup raisins

12 green cardamom pods, crushed,
pods discarded, black seeds reserved

¼ cup toasted pine nuts

2 tablespoons blanched pistachios

1–2 sheets thin silver foil (varak)
(optional, for special occasions)

**SERVES 4**

Put the butter ghee or butter into a large, wide, heavy-bottom, preferably nonstick 5-quart saucepan and heat over moderate heat. Stir-fry the rice until it darkens to pale gold, then add the bay leaves and milk. Increase the heat to high and, stirring constantly, bring to a frothing boil (about 10–12 minutes). Reduce the heat slightly to medium high.

Let the milk boil for another 35–40 minutes, until reduced to about half the original volume. Add the sugar, raisins, and cardamom. Continue to cook on a low heat, stirring often, for another 15–20 minutes, until reduced to about a third or a quarter of its original volume. Stir and cool over ice water, then chill.

Decorate with nuts and silver foil, if using, lifting the foil on its attached tissue paper, inverting it over the pudding, then pulling off the amount needed using a fine brush. The pieces do not need to be immaculate—fragments look good.

# Indian rice dessert
## with cardamom and pine nuts

India is renowned for her superb condensed milk desserts and this one is wonderful served warm, cool, or chilled. Cardamom, nuts, rosewater, or almond essence, as well as sugar in various forms, add scent. For a special occasion, top it with varak, which is real silver, hand-beaten into paper-fine sheets. It is available from Asian stores or specialist grocers and adds drama to this already exotic dish.

I make few cakes and those I do make have to be quick, effortless, and absolutely delicious. Serve slices with citrus sorbet as a dessert. Alternatively, enjoy it purely as a cake with a tiny espresso and a glass of ice water. Cointreau or Grand Marnier are excellent alternatives for the lemon liqueur.

# semolina citrus cake

Reserve a little of the grated lemon and orange zest and put the remainder into a bowl with the oil, sugar, salt, orange and lemon juice, and eggs. Beat with a hand-held electric mixer or wire whisk until light and fluffy and doubled in volume.

Sift the semolina and baking powder into a second bowl and add the ground almonds. Fold the almond essence and orange flower water, if using, into the egg mixture. Pour all at once into the dry ingredients and fold together, but do not overmix. Spoon into the prepared pan and smooth the top.

Bake towards the top of a preheated oven at 325°F for about 40–45 minutes or until pale gold at the edges and firm in the middle. A skewer pushed into the center should come out clean.

Remove from the oven and let cool in the pan for about 10 minutes. Pour the liqueur over the top. Push the cake out, still on its loose metal base, and let cool on a wire rack for another 10 minutes. Remove the base and paper. Serve in 8–12 wedges, warm or cool, but not chilled.

The cake will keep in an airtight container for up to 4 days.

**grated zest and juice of 1 lemon**

**grated zest and juice of 1 orange**

**¾ cup extra virgin olive oil**

**1 cup sugar**

**¼ teaspoon salt**

**3 large eggs**

**1½ cups semolina**

**1 teaspoon baking powder**

**1 cup ground almonds, tightly packed, or 1¼ cups slivered almonds, ground in a blender**

**1 teaspoon almond essence**

**1 teaspoon orange flower water (optional)**

**¼ cup Cointreau or Grand Marnier (or authentic Limoncello liqueur )**

*a springform cake pan, 9-inch diameter, lightly oiled and lined with parchment*

**SERVES 8–12**

This cake is made in less than ten minutes and baked in forty, so you get a spectacular result for little effort. It's made with olive oil, so you can soothe your conscience by telling yourself how healthy it is.

# greek honey, walnut, and brandy cake

½ cup extra virgin olive oil

½ cup sugar

2 large eggs

2 cups walnut pieces

1½ cups self-rising flour, sifted

¼ teaspoon salt

½ cup drained plain yogurt or thick-set yogurt

2 tablespoons brandy

2 tablespoons clear honey

*a springform cake pan, 8-inch diameter, oiled and lined with parchment paper*

**SERVES 8–12**

Put the oil, sugar, and eggs into a large bowl and beat with a hand-held electric mixer until light and fluffy. Reserve a handful of the walnut pieces for decoration and chop the remainder with a knife or food processor in brief bursts until fine, but not mealy.

Add to the bowl, together with the flour, salt, and yogurt. Using broad strokes, mix the batter with a wooden spoon until smooth and even. Do not overmix.

Spoon the mixture into the prepared cake pan and smooth flat on top. Sprinkle with the reserved nuts.

Bake towards the top of a preheated oven at 340°F for 40 minutes.

Test the center—a skewer inserted at an angle into the center should come out clean. Listen for a popping, bubbling sound, too.

Put the brandy and honey into a small bowl and stir until dissolved. Trickle the mixture over the top of the cake, then let cool in the pan for 20 minutes.

Remove the cake, still on its loose metal base, and cool on a wire rack for 10 minutes. Remove the base, peel off the paper and serve warm or cold.

The cake will keep in an airtight container for 4 days.

# index

## conversion charts

Weights and measures have been rounded up or down slightly to make measuring easier.

volume equivalents

| american | metric | imperial |
|---|---|---|
| 1 teaspoon | 5 ml | |
| 1 tablespoon | 15 ml | |
| ¼ cup | 60 ml | 2 fl.oz. |
| ⅓ cup | 75 ml | 2½ fl.oz. |
| ½ cup | 125 ml | 4 fl.oz. |
| ⅔ cup | 150 ml | 5 fl.oz. (¼ pint) |
| ¾ cup | 175 ml | 6 fl.oz. |
| 1 cup | 250 ml | 8 fl.oz. |

| weight equivalents: | | measurements: | |
|---|---|---|---|
| imperial | metric | inches | cm |
| 1 oz. | 25 g | ¼ inch | 5 mm |
| 2 oz. | 50 g | ½ inch | 1 cm |
| 3 oz. | 75 g | ¾ inch | 1.5 cm |
| 4 oz. | 125 g | 1 inch | 2.5 cm |
| 5 oz. | 150 g | 2 inches | 5 cm |
| 6 oz. | 175 g | 3 inches | 7 cm |
| 7 oz. | 200 g | 4 inches | 10 cm |
| 8 oz. | 250 g | 5 inches | 12 cm |
| 9 oz. | 275 g | 6 inches | 15 cm |
| 10 oz. | 300 g | 7 inches | 18 cm |
| 11 oz. | 325 g | 8 inches | 20 cm |
| 12 oz. | 375 g | 9 inches | 23 cm |
| 13 oz. | 400 g | 10 inches | 25 cm |
| 14 oz. | 425 g | 11 inches | 28 cm |
| 15 oz. | 475 g | 12 inches | 30 cm |
| 16 oz. (1 lb.) | 500 g | | |
| 2 lb. | 1 kg | | |

oven temperatures:

| | | |
|---|---|---|
| 225°F | 110°C | Gas ¼ |
| 250°F | 120°C | Gas ½ |
| 275°F | 140°C | Gas 1 |
| 300°F | 150°C | Gas 2 |
| 325°F | 160°C | Gas 3 |
| 350°F | 180°C | Gas 4 |
| 375°F | 190°C | Gas 5 |
| 400°F | 200°C | Gas 6 |
| 425°F | 220°C | Gas 7 |
| 450°F | 230°C | Gas 8 |
| 475°F | 240°C | Gas 9 |